PHILIP

*The Man Behind
The Monarchy*

PHILIP

*The Man Behind
The Monarchy*

UNITY HALL

MICHAEL O'MARA BOOKS LIMITED

First published in Great Britain by
Michael O'Mara Books Ltd
20 Queen Anne Street
London W1N 9FB

British Library Cataloguing in Publication Data

Hall, Unity
    Philip: the man behind the monarchy.
    1. Philip. *Prince, Consort of Elizabeth II,*
    Queen of Great Britain   2. Great Britain—
    Princes and princesses—biography
    I. Title
    941.085'092'4   DA591.A2

ISBN 0 948397 37 3

Editors: Peter Coxhead and Mary Anne Sanders
Design: Simon Bell
Picture Research: Sarah Coombe

Typeset by Florencetype Ltd, Kewstoke, Avon
Printed and bound in Great Britain
by Butler and Tanner Ltd, Frome

CONTENTS

ACKNOWLEDGEMENTS

My grateful thanks to Stuart Kuttner, John Lisners, Sharon Ring, Amanda Shrimsley, Fiona Macdonald Hull, Trevor Kempson and Stuart Payne, whose enthusiastic research made my job so much easier

PICTURE ACKNOWLEDGEMENTS

Alpha

BBC Hulton Picture Library

Camera Press

The Illustrated London News

News International Plc

The Raymond Mander and Joe Mitchenson Theatre Collection

Syndication International

Topham Picture Library

1

THE HUSBAND AND THE MAN

In public, for the past forty years, Prince Philip, the most fiercely competitive of men, has had to walk at least one pace behind his wife. Constitutionally he does not exist. He does not even formally have the title of Prince Consort, probably because he wouldn't want it. He has walked a tightrope for all his married life in what could have been an impossible role for a man of his aggressive temperament. Not only must his wife always take precedence over him, but should he outlive the Queen, his son, Charles, would leapfrog to the number one position in the monarchy.

Does he mind? He has never made his feelings on the subject clear, though some years ago he was asked by an American interviewer if he had ever thought that maybe it would be nice to be a king? Or did he feel he was glad he wasn't a king?

'I'm glad I'm not,' he said.

The interviewer asked why.

'Well, I'm not. It's a hypothetical question.'

'You mean you are making the best of your present lot?' he was asked.

'Oh, yes,' said Philip. 'But I would anyway.'

It is fortunate that the Queen is a staunch traditionalist. She believes that a man should be master in his own home and has always appreciated how difficult it is for someone so obsessed with his masculine image as her husband to be Number Two. He cannot be involved in her role and her job. Constitutionally he is forbidden to see State papers, though he was once offered the right to peruse them.

He turned it down on the grounds that it would restrict his own freedom of speech. This means that the Queen can discuss their contents with their son and her heir, the Prince of Wales, but not with her husband.

It would be foolish to suppose that she does not sometimes informally discuss State and government matters with her husband. But like her father before her she is a stickler for protocol; and lives her life by the book. While Philip does not have the right to be involved in State affairs, she would abide by the rules.

It was on his sixty-fifth birthday that Philip came nearest to baring his deeper feelings. He said: 'There's no point worrying about what might have been. Whatever the position there are advantages and disadvantages, and one balances out the other.

'I'm delighted to be where I am for a variety of reasons. At the same time I regret it for a great many other reasons.'

He refused to say what had given him the most regrets, falling back on his old excuse whenever he is asked a question he doesn't want to answer. 'It's hypothetical,' he said.

But he did add that his marriage to the Queen had been a tremendous success.

'After all, we've been living very happily as husband and wife for 38 years and that should be comment enough in itself.'

On 20 November 1987 it became forty years. The Duke of Edinburgh and the Queen celebrated their ruby wedding. Since royalty never vary their routine, it would be surprising if the day had not started with an enormous bouquet of white blooms — carnations, roses, lilies, and lilies of the valley presented by the Prince to his wife after breakfast . . . just as he has for the past forty years. The flowers have never been forgotten even on the occasions when he was away on the day of the anniversary.

Prince Philip and the Queen are now into their sixties. Quite naturally they are not quite the golden couple who enchanted the world on their wedding day, but the glamour is still there. The Queen, has, perhaps, aged the most. Recently she has begun to resemble her great great grandmother, Queen Victoria, whose sense of duty she inherited and whose life of duty she has emulated. Philip has kept his good looks and strong physique, but lost some of his youthful flaxen hair which is now more grey than gold. He is also plagued by arthritis, the pain of which shortens the fuse on his already hair-trigger temper.

Those who know them well say there is still a very deep bond of love and affection between them. They still have much to say to each other. They still make each other laugh.

But it cannot have been all roses being married to the eagle-eyed, eagle-beaked Philip. He can be impossible when things do not go his way. It was lucky for him that the Queen has what many would consider an old-fashioned view of marriage. She promised to obey at her wedding and when she was still a young woman—long before wives usually get around to realizing it—she told a friend: 'It's a waste of time trying to change a man's character. You have to accept your husband as he is.' She also said in her early thirties: 'There's nothing worse than to fence a man in and stop him from doing what he wants.'

With her approval, Philip has managed to get through life mostly doing what he wants. Her serene acceptance of the man he is has kept the marriage alive. The Queen has held her family life together by giving her husband a very long rein to follow all the way home. Within the home she has always deferred to him. 'Ask papa,' she told the children when they were small. 'I'll see what Philip thinks,' she says to friends.

He in turn has always been her greatest support, and he has always tried to protect her. He will shout where she cannot. 'Get those bloody cameras away from the Queen,' is the familiar cry. And a freezing stare from the Nordic blue eyes has stopped many a presumptious member of the public in their tracks.

The affable Ronald Allison, who became the Queen's Press Secretary in 1973 and stayed in the job for five years says: 'I've always admired the way the Duke supports the Queen. They make a very good double act. They are very close. On an engagement together the Queen would be walking down one side and Prince Philip the other, she'll be quiet and smiling and he'll be cracking jokes and livening the atmosphere.

'I think a very good way of seeing how close a couple might be is their desire to share things. A frequent memory I have of

Prince Philip is seeing him—if he'd spotted something in the crowd—drawing the Queen's attention to it. "Oh, look there, darling," he'd say, making sure she had seen it.

'If you don't like someone you don't bother to point things out. You don't care whether they see them or not.'

Do they call each other darling? Yes, though not too often in public. To him, she is the Queen in public, Lilibet, her childhood name, at home, and he is Philip, or my husband to her. Never Phil.

The Queen may be the Queen and Prince Charles the heir presumptive, but Elizabeth has always seen to it that her husband is very much the boss and the head of the royal family in their private life. Precedence in public is the Queen's. In private, it belongs to him.

Years ago, on one of the first Australian tours the Queen and he made, he was introduced to a Mr and Dr Robinson. Mr Robinson explained that his wife was a Doctor of Philosophy—'very much more important than me,' he explained.

'Ah, yes,' said the Duke, 'we have that trouble in our family, too.'

'Within the house, and whatever we did, it was together,' he once said. 'I suppose I naturally filled the principal position. People used to come to me and ask me what to do. In 1952 [after the King's death] the whole thing changed very, very considerably.'

His frustration was that before his wife was the Queen, those who worked for them were quite happy to come to him with their questions. Once she took on the mantle of Majesty, they jealously guarded their right to approach her. He felt superfluous and angry that he could not share her burdens.

'Because she's the Sovereign, everybody turns to her,' he said. 'If you have a King and a Queen, there are certain things people automatically go to the Queen about. But if the Queen is also the *Queen*, they go to her about everything. She's asked to do much more than she normally would do . . .'

Nevertheless, he has run the family and the family firm with great success. Very early in her reign, the Queen made her husband Chief Ranger of Great Windsor Park. It sounds like an honarary title, but in fact it was considerably more. The job gave Philip the chance to sharpen his teeth on estate management, something he has been deeply involved in ever since. The royal estates, Windsor—which actually belongs to the State—Sandringham and Balmoral—which are the Queen's own—were merely run as extremely expensive run-down holiday homes. It did not take long before Philip was working out ways in which to make Sandringham in particular self-supporting.

Sandringham was going to be run without pomp and ceremony and less staff because, as Prince Philip explained it, 'everyone would muck in.' And that meant the royals as well. Not surprisingly it didn't quite work out like that. The royals didn't do a lot of 'mucking in' and all that happened was that Sandringham got a dish-washer, and people came down for breakfast instead of having it served in their room.

Sandringham offered him 20,104 acres to play with, much of it let to tenant farmers. But the Queen's own 3,310 acres now produce blackcurrants for the soft drink, Ribena, pigs for bacon packaging, turkeys (the staff get one every Christmas at cost), orchids, and among other vegetables, mushrooms for market. Everything is sold. So much so that if Prince Philip wants a mushroom for his breakfast, the chef has to send out to the shops for them. And the public are invited to come and pick their own apples (at a price) each autumn.

He has also quietly reclaimed quite a few acres from the sea, adding to the size of the estate, while the Queen's own hobby of gundog-breeding also adds to the royal coffers. He eventually put new kitchens into the 270-room house. They are modern and efficient it is true, but said to be truly hideous, as are the grace and favour residences that he built for old servants in Windsor Great Park.

It is from the Home Farm at Windsor where the royal family get their cream, milk and eggs—free range, of course. The dairy produce from there is even delivered to Buckingham Palace.

His one regret concerning Balmoral and Sandringham is that both estates have public roads running through them and it is impossible to keep the public, and more important, the press, out. Scotland in particular is full of tourists who wander on to royal property and there is no way that the royals can keep them off the land. People simply took no notice of 'Private Property' or 'Keep Off' signs until the Duke had one of his brilliant ideas. He erected new signs that worked a treat. They read: 'Beware of Adders'.

Before he got going on the holiday homes, Prince Philip decided to modernize Buckingham Palace. His plans caused considerable fluttering among the older courtiers, who did not care for the changes. He brought in modern office equipment. He streamlined the system so that the chain of command from royal to page to footman to lesser footman, and finally to the kitchen or postroom—or wherever the royal wanted some action to be taken—was cut out. He also installed an intercom system.

The new machinery worked, but he never has quite managed to change the way things are done. The chain of command, with each staff member having their own role, is too ingrained to alter. But it was on his suggestion that powdered hair was done away with for the footmen—and that was definitely a popular move.

He moved things about, too, and put in false ceilings while the Ministry of Works panicked about the original old plastered cornices. He helped himself to some paintings to brighten up the corridor outside his study. When the Queen saw them hanging in place, she realized he had chosen part of the State collection from the State apartments. 'You'll get us shot!' she said. 'They belong to the State.' He had to put them back.

The Queen has always been wise enough to recognize her husband's phenomenal energy and let him get on with things. Reorganizing the Palace, along with his polo, his fund-raising and his speech-making kept him occupied for the first difficult years of her reign.

The bee in his bonnet about efficiency caused another of his early clean sweeps. He brought in Sir Basil Smallpiece, a tycoon of public industry, to find a way to make the Palace cheaper to run. They decided on a time and study motion to see how hard everyone worked and which staff were needed and which were not.

The most worried member of the staff was the Duke's own page. On the occasions when the Duke was away, he had absolutely nothing to do. But God was in his corner. Hearing that the Duke would be in London for a week, he suggested to the time-study men that perhaps they would like to time him.

For the week that the Duke was at home, they recorded his page's every movement. He was a very busy man, rushed off his feet until the Duke departed again. When the time and motion report was returned to the Palace it had one particular recommendation. They felt that the Duke of Edinburgh's page required some extra help!

It is true that because he is away so much the Duke's pages and footmen are either worked to death or have absolutely nothing to do. When he does return to the Palace, there is so much work to be done in the short time before he disappears again that by the time he does leave everyone is exhausted.

His personal staff get paranoid because they see him so rarely and when they do, he is always shouting at them. But being used to him, and knowing that his bark is worse than his bite, they don't take a lot of notice and behind his back refer to him as 'father'.

Royalty get attached to their staff and don't like change. The Duke was most distressed when two of his valets died from heart attacks, one in most dramatic circumstances. The Queen and the Duke were guests at Lord Dalhousie's estate in Scotland and out shooting. The valet, Joe Pearce, who had been with the royal family for many years was acting as Philip's loader.

The Queen was behind, watching with binoculars, working the dogs and picking up the shot grouse. She saw a figure fall. For one moment she thought it was the Duke and ran as fast as she could to where the two men were.

The Duke was fine, but Joe Pearce was dead.

Philip had his body sent home to the north, and a special memorial service was arranged at St James's, Piccadilly, which he attended.

He is used to the number of gays about the Palace, but they often offend his macho soul. He noticed that one particular footman had been missing for a few days and asked his page where he had got to?

'He was sacked, sir,' he was told.

Philip wanted to know what he had done.

'I'm afraid they found him in bed with one of the housemaids, sir,' the page said.

'And they sacked him!' the Duke said, outraged. 'The man should have been given a medal.'

In the fifties and sixties there was a great deal of comment about the fact that Edinburgh was so rarely at home and that the Queen and he were apart so much of the time. He still is away more often than not, but somehow it does not seem as remarkable as when he was younger. He likes to roam and is a natural traveller. He'll take any excuse to go anywhere as long as it's not costing anything and particularly if it is somehwere he has not been before. He travels around 75,000 miles a year, often piloting himself. The Queen once sighed: 'If he takes on any more, he soon won't be here for breakfast!'

In fact, he often isn't there for breakfast. He wasn't there the morning that Michael Fagan paid his early morning call on the Queen after breaking into the Palace and no one has quite established exactly where he was. The Queen, woken at 7.18 am by a young man in jeans, a broken glass ashtray in his hand, and dripping blood, had to get herself out of that one, since the policeman who was supposed to be on duty in the corridor outside her room wasn't. Nor was the night alarm bell by her bed working.

The Fagan affair had one good result. The Duke is pathological about having policemen anywhere near him and the Queen. He believes that too much security is self-defeating. On the grouse moors, he roars at the unfortunate members of the force who have to accompany him to get out of his sight. Plans were going ahead to have the police house at Balmoral enlarged until Philip stepped in and said bluntly that he would not have seventy-odd policemen living at the bottom of the garden. After the Fagan episode, he was left with a goose-sized egg on his face, and security was tightened up with less protest from him.

He has few close friends whereas the Queen has many. He is not an easy friend to have since it is necessary to agree with him. He can get pretty salty if people do not go along with his viewpoint. This does not make for cosy dinner parties, and requires that his guests—or indeed his hosts—have to keep their lip buttoned and their opinions to themselves. He is as capable of being rude in private as he is in public. And the Queen has been heard to say to her guests who are brave enough to argue with him: 'That's right! You tell him!'

Holding such strong opinions, he enjoys making speeches. Out can pour his views, with no one to answer back. And his speeches, though just occasionally a bit daft—well, it was daft to say he had little sympathy for the unemployed!—are entertaining and do not send the audience to sleep over the brandy. And he is capable of being sharply to the point. Many of his speeches over the years might have offended people, but they have also made them think.

Many nights of his life, when he is not on holiday, he is making a speech. While the Queen dines alone at the Palace, perfectly content with her own company, if she bothered to look out of her window she could probably spot at which Mayfair hotel he was spouting that night.

He has spent his life being controversial, but the Queen is not permitted to be. On one occasion at dinner when the conversation became a little politically sensitive, the Duke asked the Queen for her opinion.

She immediately looked under the table where the corgis hide at mealtimes and called: 'Sugar, Sugar, where are you, Sugar?'

'That,' said Philip dryly, 'is Lilibet's dog defence mechanism going into play. If she doesn't want to commit herself, she calls the dogs.'

He and his wife don't always like the same things. She isn't much interested in his carriage driving or sailing, though she learned to like watching polo over the years, which is just as well. She now has to watch her eldest son play it. Prince Philip cannot abide horse-racing, which is probably his wife's favourite pastime. In fact, being a 'doing' man he doesn't care for spectator sports at all. He endures the carriage ride around the racecourse on Royal Ascot week but takes himself to a small private room in the Queen's box where he watches cricket on the television for the rest of the day.

They do bicker gently over things that the rest of us would

9

hardly credit. In Paris, on a State visit in the seventies they were dining alone, except for the regulation page and footman, before going on to a reception. A British military band was playing outside. The Duke, listening carefully, said: 'Oh, that's my regiment.'

'It is not,' said the Queen, 'it's mine.'

It was. They all are.

When they have a tiff, they walk in silence to the waiting car, but indoors, voices have been heard to be raised. They have their quarrels like anyone else. She says his temper can be almost unbearable. He once threatened to make her walk home from a polo match at Windsor because she complained about his driving. She no doubt had cause. He is an aggressive driver who generally goes too fast. Though she is a very good and careful driver, he *always* drives the car on their own private lands and she has 'learnt to draw breath only silently.' He was probably annoyed with her the morning when he was leaving for an engagement, and, uncharacteristically, the Queen was late leaving for an engagement of her own. As Philip appeared, her worried chauffeur asked him when the Queen would be leaving. 'How the bloody hell would I know!' snapped Philip.

Yet conversely, she never gets annoyed with him in public, except once, many years ago, when she was inspecting the Home Fleet. Philip, no doubt remembering his own navy days, found the temptation not to follow protocol and not remain the regulation step behind the Sovereign irresistible. He stayed so far behind as to appear not to be with her at all. He lagged on every ship, sometimes as much as forty yards, as he stopped to question officers and ratings.

Aboard *Ocean* he became engrossed in conversation with a rating and kept the Queen waiting, her foot just gently tapping and on the aircraft carrier *Albion*, the Queen said to the Commanding Officer, Captain R.M. Smeaton: 'I suppose we'll have to wait for Philip again. He really is the limit.'

The captain sent across a danger signal, and Philip sensing the atmosphere, cut across the flight deck to join the main party.

Whatever Philip does it has never affected the deepness of their relationship. He has been good for the Queen. She was a solemn girl, always anxious about doing the right things, and concerned that everyone around her was happy. She is a thoroughly un-selfish human being, and among those who work for royalty, she is everyone's favourite. She's human enough to enjoy a bit of gossip—something that her husband can't abide. But in the early days of their marriage, he chirped her up no end. She had never been much of a one for games or physical exercise, but he made her walk and play softball. He also made her laugh. In early days at the Palace, the staff heard screams of royal laughter. It was Philip, chasing his wife down the corridor wearing a pair of hideous, joke false teeth.

When she made her first TV broadcast, he sent a message to her via the producer. It was 'Tell the Queen to remember the wailing and gnashing of teeth.' Nobody understood except the Queen. When the message was passed on she immediately smiled and relaxed.

But it has never been what most of us would consider a normal marriage. It seems to have worked on a basis of separation. He has never been at home a lot, other than at their very long holiday times. And they have never slept in the same bedroom and shared the same bed—not since the honeymoon when they slept at Broadlands in Lord and Lady Mountbatten's bedroom with Dali drawings on the walls. All their married life they have had interconnecting rooms.

His opinion is important to her. Like most husbands he doesn't take a lot of notice of what she is wearing but occasionally he will spot something new and comment. When he does, people have noticed that the Queen goes slightly pink and looks inordinately pleased.

A clue to this complicated man lies in his personal study. It should be, like him, a model of efficiency, organization and tidiness. It is, in fact, in a state of clutter, with his oil paintings stacked up against the wall, his newest inventions peppered over his desk, and with his papers cluttered willy-nilly where only he could possibly find them.

Apart from his carriage driving, his only other hobby is collecting walking sticks. A whole room at Windsor has been turned over to them. It would be a tragedy for the royal family if his arthritis forced him to use them. Already it takes him a great effort of will—and pain-killers—to get into his carriage and four.

It is said that arthritis is a stress disease. The only other illness that ever troubles him is jaundice, but then he is inclined to be a bit liverish at the best of times. Certainly the Duke has lived a stressful life—of his own choosing. But has it been a happy one? Remembering his words: 'I am delighted to be where I am for a variety of reasons. At the same time I regret it for a great many other reasons,' one wonders what are those regrets. He is unlikely to tell us. Particularly as, looking back at history, it is now clear that the life he leads is the one he quite consciously chose for himself. And at a very early age.

2

THE MAKING OF
THE MAN

It was on the 10 June 1921 that Prince Philip was born on the island of Corfu. He was delivered on the dining-room table of a Regency-style villa, quaintly named 'Mon Repos', which his mother and father, Prince and Princess Andrew of Greece, then owned.

He was an after-thought baby, youngest of five and the only boy. His nearest sister, Sophie was 7 at the time of his birth and his mother, Princess Andrew of Greece, at 36 was no longer a young woman.

The Princess had been married for eighteen years when she found herself pregnant again. When her labour pains began the local doctor decided that her bed was not suitable for the birth. He carried her downstairs, and the *accouchement* of the future British consort took place on the dining-room table. Some say on a white embroidered tablecloth—an interesting variation on the silver spoon theme. But then, silver spoons were always conspicuous by their absence in Prince Philip's immediate family. His parents were royal but of meagre means. The imposing house where Philip was born had the most charming garden tumbling down to the cliffs, but inside there was no electricity or gas, no running hot water, and no heating. The Andrews did not live like royalty because they could not afford to do so.

There had been anxieties about the birth because the Princess had been under considerable strain. For three years after the ending of the Great War she, with King Constantine and the rest of the Greek royal family, had been exiled to Switzerland. Their

13

private income had been stopped by the Greek Government and they had been forced to live on borrowed money, never knowing from where the next quarter's rent was coming.

There was a puppet king on the throne of Greece, Alexander I, Constantine's second son. It was his death in 1920, aged 27, bizarrely from a pet monkey's bite, that caused a plebiscite to be held in Greece. To the dismay of the Greek revolutionary government and the astonishment of the governments of most of Europe, the majority of the people voted for the return of the monarchy. Therefore, when Prince Philip was born, King Constantine had just scraped back onto his throne in Athens, and Princess Andrew of Greece, heavily pregnant, was back home on Corfu. But not with her husband. At the express wish of his brother, the King, Andrew was to go to war, leading a Greek infantry division against the Turks in Asia Minor. It was a hopeless battle and he was aware it could never be won.

Philip's English-born mother, Princess Alice of Battenberg, was the daughter of the first Marquis of Milford Haven and sister to Lord Louis Mountbatten. She was a truly stunning beauty, but had been born with a severe hearing impediment. However, since she could lip-read in four languages, her deafness caused her little difficulty. And her hearing problems certainly never troubled Prince Philip's father. He saw her flaxen hair and delicate face and courted her from their first meeting at the coronation of Britain's King Edward VII in 1901. She was 17 and he was 20 and not much more than a year elapsed before they were married.

He was an elegant, young cavalry officer with great style and much charm. He wore his monocle jauntily and, like his son, enjoyed a joke and making people laugh. He was also something of a dandy. A hard-up dandy. His father King George I of the Hellenes had seven children and no money, and for this reason King Edward VII, Alice's great-uncle, did not think this at all a suitable romance for the prettiest princess in all Europe. Nor, indeed did Alice's father Prince Louis of Battenburg. He was Director of Naval Intelligence at the Admiralty and though not a particularly rich man, he was still considerably more comfortably off than Prince Andrew.

Prince Andrew, with a touch of grandeur, insisted that he could take care of his wife on his officer's pay. But it was a frivolous suggestion. Though Alice was frugal by nature, he was not. They were always to have financial troubles, yet even in the grimmest hours, Prince Andrew could not bring himself to surrender his valet.

But the Princess Alice wanted him, as years later another Princess, the Princess Elizabeth, would want her only son. And objections to the marriage ceased when several imperial and royal relatives between them 'donated sufficient funds for the young people to start married life without excessive financial sorrows.' It was said that the Tsar of Russia's contribution was a staggering (and unlikely) £100,000. But however much it was, it wasn't enough to enable Philip's parents and their children to live with any more style than the family of a British bank manager of the day.

Leaving his new baby son, Philip's father went off to the wars to serve his country. He returned to 'Mon Repos' in October 1922. He had been relieved of his command at his own request. The war was disastrously lost and Prince Andrew's troops, helpless without modern weaponry, had been the first to crack against the ferocity of the Turks. King Constantine was forced to abdicate for the second time and his brother, George, took over the tottering throne.

Prince Andrew had hardly been home five minutes when a destroyer arrived to take him to Athens. He left Corfu willingly enough, thinking that his old school friend, Theodorus Pangalos, the Minister of War, required him to give his version of the humiliating defeat that Greece had suffered at the hands of the Turks. Once in the capital he found himself immediately imprisoned on charges of disobedience and desertion. A calamity of the magnitude of the Greek defeat, in which thousands of the Greek soldiers and their countrymen living in Asia Minor had been slaughtered, required scapegoats. Three ex-prime ministers, other ministers, generals and officers were already in prison. But what better scapegoat for a revolutionary-minded Government than a royal officer? Prince Andrew was indicted for high treason and accused with the others of responsibility for the Greek defeat.

At the first of the trials, the six accused were all found guilty and without any messing about, executed by firing squad the following morning, 13 November.

It was fortunate that Philip's father was in the second group to be tried, for the delay—and Princess Andrew—saved him. She left her children in the care of their English Nanny Roose and travelled to Athens in an attempt to rescue her husband. She appealed to the new King, but he was virtually a prisoner in his own palace and had no power. She appealed to the Pope, to King Alphonso of Spain, to the President of France and to the King of Great Britain and Northern Ireland.

Her chances of success were slight. The Greek royal family were believed to have been pro-German in the war and contemptuously called 'the German Greeks'. Their popularity was at an all-time low in Western Europe. Princess Andrew received messages of sympathy, and little else. Except from Britain.

Her brother, Lord Louis Mountbatten (Prince Philip's Uncle Dickie), was a close friend of the Prince of Wales. Together they lobbied King George V for help in rescuing Uncle Andrew.

The King did not need much persuasion. He became fired with the idea of a rescue and a Foreign Office telegram arrived at the British Legation in Greece saying: 'The King is most anxious concerning Prince Andrew. Please report on his Royal Highness's present position and keep us informed by telegraph of any developments.'

Andrew's present position was not good. Pangalos, the instigator of his trial, visited him in jail.

'How many children have you?' he asked suddenly.

'Five,' said Prince Andrew.

Pangalos shook his head.

'Poor things, they will soon be orphans,' he said.

No one was allowed near the Prince—except his valet. Prince Christopher, his youngest brother, had rushed to Athens from Paris to try to help. He was permitted to stay for about eight days, but he got nowhere. He was even refused permission to see his brother. No letters, no parcels were allowed in or out of the prison.

Christopher hit upon the idea of writing a letter on cigarette paper, rolling it tightly and putting it into the valet's cigarette case. He received a brave letter back, but containing no hope. Prince Andrew, Pangalos's words ringing in his ears, was waiting philosophically for death.

But events were moving in England. Commander Gerald Talbot, a British agent who had at one time been Britain's naval attaché in Athens, was told to get Prince Andrew and his family out of Greece—somehow. He had only one day in which to succeed.

If the worst came to the worst, the commander planned to abduct them all in true James Bond fashion. But he knew Pangalos of old from his Athens service, and having slid into Greece cloak-and-dagger fashion with false papers and using a disguise, he went to see the Minister of War.

The interview did not go well. Pangalos was refusing to give any quarter but as he dramatically insisted that Prince Andrew must die, an aide rushed into the room.

'Sir,' he stammered, 'there is a British warship in the bay.'

There was indeed, the HMS *Calypso*, and with her guns raised threateningly upright. She was there because King George V himself had picked up the Buckingham Palace telephone and, exercising a rarely used royal prerogative, had personally requested that a warship be sent to aid Commander Talbot in his mission.

The atmosphere in Pangalos's office changed. Serious talking began. Commander Talbot was able to extract a promise from the Minister of War and the other revolutionary leader of the Government, Colonel Plastiras (who had actually served under Prince Andrew), that the Prince would not be executed.

He would be tried on Saturday, the next morning, and sentenced to penal servitude, or possibly death. Plastiras would then grant a pardon and he would be handed to Commander Talbot for immediate removal from the country by HMS *Calypso*.

That afternoon Talbot had a message sent from the British Legation in Athens to the Foreign Office. '. . . British warship must be at Phaleron by midday December 3rd and captain should report immediately to legation for orders, but in view of necessity

17

for utmost secrecy, captain should be given no indication of reason for voyage.

'This promise has been obtained with greatest difficulty and Talbot is convinced that above arrangement be strictly adhered to so as to save Prince's life. As success of plan depends on absolute secrecy of existence of this arrangement, even Prince and Princess cannot be given hint of coming. Talbot is convinced he can rely on word given him, and I see of no other possibility of saving Prince's life.'

Andrew's fellow prisoners were condemned and executed. The court found Prince Andrew guilty of the disgrace of disobeying orders and abandoning his post, sentencing him to imprisonment, deprivation of rank and titles and banishment from Greece for life.

But, added the judgement, 'consideration being given to extenuating circumstances of lack of experience in commanding a large unit, he has been degraded and condemned to perpetual banishment.'

Those words seered in Prince Andrew's soul. They were untrue, but they had saved his life and dealt his honour a death blow. He would never live in Greece again.

During that night Pangalos arrived at the prison with Talbot, and personally drove them both to join HMS *Calypso*, where a relieved Princess Andrew was already waiting on board. Captain Buchanan-Wollaston then steamed for Corfu, where the four little girls and the 18-month old Prince Philip, in his nanny's arms, were taken aboard the cruiser. Too small for a bunk, the ship's carpenter set about making a cot for the baby out of a padded orange box. It is said that he took his first steps on the deck of HMS *Calypso*. It was his first experience of the Royal Navy and perhaps the reason why in later years he joined the British— rather than the Greek—naval service.

Once the ship was steaming for Brindisi and safety, Captain Buchanan-Wollaston thought to himself that this particular royal family seemed quite philosophical about being exiled . . . 'for they so frequently are'.

From the time that Philip's father was exiled from Greece, the family never had a home of their own again, although they were always able to find a roof under which to shelter. They had hardly any money, but if some other more secure member of the sprawling family did not pick up the bills, there was always a wealthy, ardent royalist who would be proud to do so. Family and royalists between them provided homes, holidays and paid the children's school fees.

As the years went by, his parent's marriage ended undramatically. It simply faded away; the couple just drifted apart. They never divorced—for royalty did not divorce in those days—but they lived apart for many years. It was an understandable decision, for in later life they had absolutely nothing in common.

The Princess became an austere religious. The Prince chose to live out his life in the sunshine of the Riviera, with something in an icebucket at his side and with Madame Andrée de la Bigne as his constant companion. She was an extremely attractive French woman and a wealthy widow who owned a small yacht, the *Davida*, on which Andrew lived for some time. Madame de la Bigne had once had a brief career as an actress, and with her Prince Andrew seemed to find contentment.

His wife found a different kind of contentment. In 1949 she created her own religious order, the Christian Sisterhood of Martha and Mary, on a Greek island. There she devoted herself to good works under a hotter, less sophisticated sun. And from the time Philip went to junior school in England, neither of them had a great deal to do with the upbringing of their only son.

Prince Philip's childhood was therefore very different from the settled life of his own four children. After the flight from Greece, the family settled for a while in Kensington Palace with Princess Alice's mother, the Dowager Duchess of Milford Haven. The Christmas there was a happy one for the children. Philip had the companionship of the 3-year-old David Milford Haven who was to become his greatest friend. Also in the nursery was Iris Mountbatten, the Marquess of Carisbrooke's little girl, just a few months older than Philip. All the grown-up Mountbattens were there, including Lord Louis, just back from honeymoon with his wife, the fabulously wealthy Edwina. In the New Year the children were left in their nanny's care while their parents went to New York to stay with brother Christopher. He had married the

19

widow of an American millionaire and they were to cruise in the family yacht from Canada to Palm Beach.

The problem of how to maintain the family was temporarily put to one side. They had all been given Danish passports by Andrew's cousin, King Christian X of Denmark. This made sense since the Greek royal family were originally Danish born.

The passport was a help. It was necessary to have a passport, but it was more necessary to have money. All Prince Andrew had was the rent from a small agricultural property in Greece, and a tiny inheritance from his father. King George V, having saved his cousin from the firing squad, is said to have declared that 'he would not pay for any extravagance Andrew might indulge in.' For Andrew was indeed extravagant—a trait which his only son has *not* inherited.

It was Uncle George of Milford Haven who coughed up for the children's school fees, and it was Uncle Prince George of Greece, Andrew's brother, who gave them all a home in Paris. Like most of the men in Philip's family, Prince George had also married extremely well. His wife was Princess Marie Bonaparte, a descendant of Napoleon, and a very wealthy woman indeed. Her father was the man who founded the casino at Monte Carlo.

The children's life was in no way deprived. They saw little of their parents, true, but there was solid, steady Nanny Roose and the equally solid housekeeper, another intrepid Englishwoman, Mrs Blower, both sticking firmly to their old-fashioned English ways. They fed the children on nourishing rice and cooked tapioca puddings instead of that nasty foreign Greek/French/German muck! as they thought of Continental food. 'Roosie' as the children called her, had already nursed Philip's cousins, the three daughters of Prince Nicholas, one of whom was Marina, the future Duchess of Kent, and Roosie believed firmly in the British way of doing things. Weeks before Philip's birth, her demands for British soap, British baby food and British baby woollies had been filled by Lord Louis Mountbatten, Princess Alice's younger brother. But he was started off on goat's milk as Corfu had no clean cow's milk.

Philip shared his nursery with Nanny Roose, and as a tiny baby he had few toys. He played with some rough bricks that the Corfu handyman had made, and liked pulling the pins in and out of a pin cushion. He was a cheerful, if naughty little boy who liked his own way. Which is maybe where his grandson, Prince William gets it from! Like most small boys he enjoyed running around banging an empty tin with a big stick. Something some might say he has continued to do for a large part of his life.

In Paris, he first lived in rooms in part of the huge mansion close to the Bois de Boulogne where Prince George and Princess Marie lived. Soon Uncle George moved his brother's family to a property near St Cloud, a small lodge attached to the big house, which they were able to regard as their own.

Philip grew to be an extrovert little boy, much loved by his four older sisters, though he could be a small aggressive bossy monster. They, in turn, formed a petticoat government to keep him in order. In no way was he a pathetic little orphan. He was a great communicator even as a small child—which was as well as his life was an endless round of visits to castles, palaces, stately homes, visiting royal relatives in Sweden, Germany, Romania, and England. In England he often stayed at Broadlands, the Mountbatten home in Hampshire. He was to stay there much later as a grown man—with his new wife, Princess Elizabeth, on their honeymoon.

But back in the 1920s, if the royal relatives did not come up trumps with holiday invitations, there were always the ardent royalists. Strongest of these supporters were the wealthy Foufounis family, Greek exiles themselves, and fortunately extremely rich. Madame Foufounis was an old friend of Princess Andrew and lived with her husband and three children in a beautiful country house with its own farm near Marseilles. They also owned a holiday home at bracing, windy Berck Plage, near Le Touquet. The Marseilles farm and surrounding sunny countryside, and the huge sandy beaches of Berck were paradise for children and Philip, Miss Roose and his sisters were regular visitors to both homes.

Helene Foufounis was to become his great friend in the future, though she was four years older than Philip. In Britain in the 1960s she became famous as Helene Cordet, cabaret star. Today she is an elegant 70-year-old woman living in Lausanne, and she remembers the small Philip very well and, still a royalist, delights in talking about him.

'His family were not really poor,' Helene, who was destined to know true poverty says. 'They had been given a house by Marie Bonaparte and they lived very well. My grandfather was a royalist and had been exiled at the same time as the King, and our family helped them very much at that time. Very much financially. They also worked for the royal family to go back to Greece. Philip has good memories of those times, and has remained a faithful friend.

'We spoke English, Philip and I, when we first met because of our English nannies. We had our bedroom doors open when we were small and Philip and I would be in adjoining rooms. I used to hear him say things in a really baby voice like: "Nanny, I want a banana." He was only three. I would mimic him, and my nanny would then mimic me.

'I was very jealous of him when he was a small boy. I don't think he disliked me as much as I disliked him, but my feelings were more jealousy than anything. Everyone adored him so much, particularly my mother, because he was so good looking. My father had died when I was very small and I felt as if I wasn't loved by my stepfather, and was the least loved of all my family. So when this blond, blue-eyed German-looking little boy came along, and my mother paid so much attention to him, I was livid. And he and my brother Iaini, used to gang up on me.'

Like small boys, rich or poor, Philip and his friend Iaini were trouble. In Marseilles they were caught trying to sell off the family Persian rugs from door to door, fortunately before they had made a sale. Once they smashed a huge flowerpot after having been warned by the Governess to take care.

'My brother was sent to his room and our Governess was looking for Philip when suddenly I saw a blue eye at the shutter outside, whispering for Iaini to run for it,' Helene recalls. 'The Governess saw him too and advanced on him. Philip knew he would be in for a spanking and he used his royal prerogative. "I get my spanking from Roosie," he told her in a haughty way.

'He was very aware of his position, and we were too. You could not forget who he was. He had been brought up to realize he was a Prince, but he was not snooty. My mother, who adored him,

22

told him she had dreams of him going back to Greece as King. He said he didn't want to go back to Greece. He was like an English boy rather than Greek or German. He had an English nanny, spoke English, had been brought up with English customs. Later, I never heard him refer to Germany except to speak of his sisters who had all married Germans.

'Though I do remember once, when we were playing, he held a Greek flag and we all sang the Greek national anthem.

'Another game we played was "the king, the servants and the pig". He never wanted to be the king, he'd rather be the pig. It was funny. We used to fight because he wouldn't be the king.

'In spite of my jealousy, I thought he was a very nice little boy. One of my cousins came to visit when she was 12 and she was very taken by Philip. She had a lot of money—she came from a very wealthy family. She took us down to the park to buy us toys. We all came back with something but there was nothing for my sick sister, Ria, who had a diseased hip. My friend said, cruelly: "I didn't buy you anything because you can't play".

'My sister was only about nine, and Philip went very red and ran out of the room. He came back with an armful of his own toys, and the new one, thrust them on her bed and said: "These are for you".

'He never did anything vicious or nasty. And he could behave well, particularly at table. We had an enormous table and I remember, one day, a lunch when Philip's parents were there and everyone was talking. We children could not talk. We had to be seen and not heard. Suddenly I saw Philip take his plate and go off to the downstairs kitchen. The cook was delighted to see him, but without a word he put his plate on the servant's table, sat down and started to eat. Marie, the maid and the cook were chatting, chat, chat, chat. He put his knife and fork down and said wearily: "Not you, too, Marie!" He'd gone downstairs to get a bit of peace and quiet.

'Another time at table, Nanny Roose had a little dribble on her nose. With us children, she used to call it "Johnny's at the door". Suddenly I heard Philip say: "Nanny . . . "

"Stop talking, Philip," she said.

"But Nanny, Johnny's at the door."

23

Nanny took no notice and then he sighed and said: "But, Nanny, Johnny's in the soup!"

'We were never allowed to talk or interrupt. Our nannies were very strict. In fact, when we were naughty we used to get beaten quite a lot. Spanking was very commonplace.'

The Foufounis were very well off at the time; rich enough to pick up the tab for Prince Andrew and his family. It was a privileged life of nannies and governesses. But it did not last. When Helene was about 11, Prince Philip went out of her life, at much the same time as the business that supported the family went bankrupt. There was, it must be said, no connection between the two events. Madame Foufounis was left to live on her capital. An extravagant woman, she spent the money on properties and continued with the same life style that she had always known. By the time Helene was 18, there was nothing left. It was many years before Helene and Prince Philip were to meet again and when they did, their circumstances had completely reversed. But Madame Foufounis clung to the friendship, sometimes against the odds of the grown Philip's arrogance and impatience. She wrote to him in 1959 to wish him and his family Happy Christmas, wondering whether or not she should. Then she assured him that she would not rush to congratulate him when the baby (Prince Andrew) arrived, and would not send the baby garments that she had had prepared 'for fear of . . . being told off! So, I am keeping away,' she promised.

Madame Foufounis had obviously transgressed.

Another childhood friend who has a similar tale to tell is Queen Alexandra of Yugoslavia. She is Philip's cousin, and was born Princess Alexandra of Greece. The daughter of the unfortunate puppet King Alexander who died from a pet monkey bite, she came into the world three months after his death and so never knew her father.

Again the rambling structure of European royalty ensured that her childhood, like Philip's was a happy one. She and he visited the same relatives, were friendly with the same royalist families and lived much the same life.

Alexandra's first memories of her cousin are of a tiny boy, shrimping net in hand, rushing towards the sea. Once in the sea he would refuse to leave it, until he was finally cornered by nanny and dragged out, blue with cold and shouting protests through chattering teeth. He loved the sea and would often rush in fully dressed before Nanny Roose could catch him.

Nanny Roose spent a great deal of her time chasing the young Prince Philip. Escaping from the bathroom, just at the moment when Nanny was testing the bathwater, was a favourite pastime. He would tear naked through the corridors of some castle or another with his 70-year-old Nanny in not so hot pursuit until someone caught him and carried him back to bath and bed.

A picture emerges of a normally naughty small boy, daredevil, climbing trees, boating, climbing on to the big farmyard horses his legs could scarcely straddle, and small heels kicking its side, ride off. He liked to balance along the railings of the farm pigsties not caring if he fell in the mire. That made it more fun and Nanny was cross. He and his cousin once released all the pigs in the middle of a grown-up's tea party. Encouraged by a stick that Philip used to goad them, they fled squealing from their sties and on to the tea lawn, creating havoc.

It was a wonderful childhood of enchanted summers in sumptuous surroundings all over Europe with masses of other little top-drawer cousins to play with.

At that time he was much more a child of his father's family than a Mountbatten. The Mountbatten influence came later.

British royal children are not brought up to think of themselves as Princes or Princesses. The Buckingham Palace rules are that children are called by their first names, and not until they reach puberty are they addressed as HRH. The Queen tried to bring her children up for as long as possible without them being aware of their own importance—if importance it is. Their father, however, was trained to think of himself as a Prince. And all through his childhood and his adult life he stubbornly insisted on referring to himself simply as Philip in the royal manner, or if pressed for a surname, Philip of Greece. The title was perhaps more important because of the family's straitened circumstances, and he was never encouraged to forget it.

He was first sent to school in Paris at the age of 6. His mother chose the American MacJannet Country Day and Boarding

School at St Cloud because she wanted her son to have his future in an English-speaking country. The school was better known as 'The Elms' from the trees that surrounded it and had once been the house of Jules Verne. This was a progressive kindergarten for the children of the rich, and it was Uncle Christopher's wife, the millionaire American auntie-in-law who paid the school-fees. The pupils were either the children of American diplomats and businessmen in Paris, or like Philip himself, small, displaced fragments of the aristocracy.

He was one of the less well-off children at The Elms and always saving up for something. He wanted a bicycle and a new mackintosh and he bought these himself. His uncle, the King of Sweden, obligingly sent him £1 every Christmas, and this was the basis of his savings. His clothes were often patched and darned, but this was more his mother's sense of thrift than real hardship. He was brought up to be thrifty and is still so today.

Already, at so young an age, he insisted to his teachers that he was Philip of Greece, and with no other name, in spite of the Danish passport that listed him as a Glücksburg. He was not a particularly brilliant pupil, just average, but with some advantages. His mother had already taught him to read, though he could not write at all. He could also speak German and English and was becoming proficient in French.

He was a boisterous little chap with nice manners and a grown-up air about him. He was inclined to show off, and liked taking charge, appointing himself class monitor. This did not prevent his fellow pupils and teachers liking him and they were sad when he left to go to his English prep school.

This was to be Cheam, where he later sent Prince Charles, making his son the first future King of England to be given a formal education. Philip went there on the advice of his mother's brother, George, Marquis of Milford Haven. The family at St Cloud was breaking up. The parents were beginning to drift apart and this may have been the cause of Philip's younger sister Sophie's unwise marriage at the age of 16. Her husband was Christopher of Hesse and, unusually for a nobleman, Christopher was an ardent Nazi. Her departure set the wedding bells ringing. By the end of 1931 all four of Philip's sisters had made good

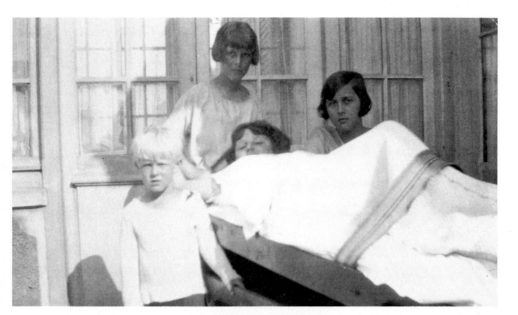

(above) The four year old Prince Philip with his sisters, Cecile and Tiny, at the Berck Plage summer house of Madame Foufounis, Helene Cordet's mother. The child in the bed, is Helene Cordet's sister, Ria, who suffered from a diseased hip. Prince Philip once gave her all his toys.

(left) The prettiest Princess in all of Europe . . . Prince Philip's mother, Alice, grand-daughter to Queen Victoria and the daughter of the first Marquis of Milford Haven. Prince Philip's father, Prince Andrew of Greece fell wildly in love with her at first sight.

(above) Prince Andrew of Greece, who was dramatically saved from a firing squad by King George V of England. He fled to Britain with his family, and lived out his life in the flesh-pots of Europe.

(opposite) Prince Philip, aged nine, in his national costume. Christened 'Phil the Greek' by the Express Newspapers when his engagement to the Princess Elizabeth was announced, the name has stuck. Even some members of the Royal family still use it—behind his back of course.

Philip 1930

Philip, tall and gangly, has the ball. Aged 14 at Gordonstoun, he was captain of the school cricket team.

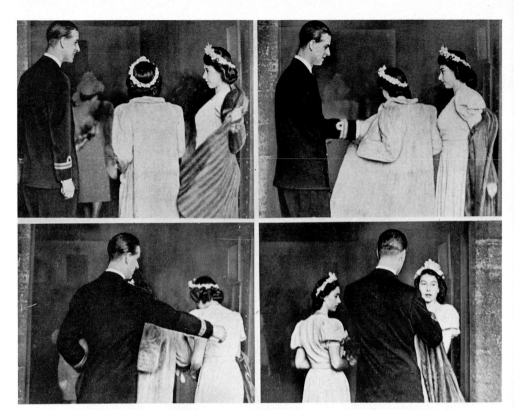

(above) Lord Mountbatten flew in from India for the wedding of his nephew, Prince Philip to the future Queen. He was met by the best man, the Marquis of Milford Haven. Later, Philip was to reject them both.

(opposite above) 1946, and Princess Elizabeth, aged 20 is bridesmaid at the wedding of Patricia Mountbatten, daughter of Lord Louis Mountbatten. Prince Philip, acting as an usher, takes his future wife's coat as she arrives at Romsey Abbey. With Princess Margaret standing between them, it was the first photograph of them together.

(opposite below) A happy Uncle Dickie Mountbatten dominates Prince Philip's stag night at the Dorchester Hotel with Michael Parker (centre).

(left) The honeymoon at Broadlands in Hampshire was not as happy as this official picture suggests. Philip was angry with the public and the press who invaded the newlywed's privacy. They moved to Balmoral in Scotland where Philip caught a cold!

(below) At Prince Philip's first home, Clarence House, in the Mall, the Queen's desk carries her favourite picture of the Duke — sporting a wartime beard. It is the picture that she kept in her sitting room at Buckingham Palace before their engagement was announced. The other pictures are of her grandmother, Queen Mary, her mother, the Queen Mother, Prince Charles as a baby, and Princess Elizabeth along with other chosen pictures of her husband.

marriages to German princelings who, in spite of the Great War, had managed to hang on to their lands, their castles and their money.

With the children gone, the home in Paris broke up. For a while Philip's mother, who was in poor health, went to live with her daughters in Germany. Eventually she returned to Greece and her life of good works, while her husband drifted to the fleshpots of Monte Carlo and the company of his widow friend.

It was Princess Andrew's elder brother, George, the Marquis of Milford Haven, who took the 8-year-old Philip under his wing and gave him a home in England. At first Philip stayed with his maternal grandmother, the Dowager Duchess of Milford Haven, but she found him too boisterous to cope with, particularly when he bought a toy saxophone. Uncle George took over and at the age of 8 he was welcomed to Lynden Manor on the Thames, near Maidenhead. It made more sense for Philip to live with George's family as his son, David, was just two years older than Philip. The two boys became great friends, sneaking off at night to canoe down rivers, and when they were in London, climbing the roofs of Kensington Palace and refusing to come down. Philip lost a tooth roller-skating in an old barn at Lynden where they played their rougher games. It was a friendship that would survive for many years.

It irritates Prince Philip that people think that Lord Louis Mountbatten—his Uncle Dickie—was his father, or indeed that Dickie was responsible for his upbringing. Given the opportunity, Philip is at pains to point out that it was George, a man with all the Mountbatten charm but minus his brother's pushiness, who was his mentor in England. It was George who turned up at school prize days, and it was more likely George, who as a sailor had fought under Jellicoe and Beatty, who talked to him of the sea and ships. And it was Uncle George, who had been at Cheam school himself, who sent Philip there and paid his school fees.

At Cheam he was again an average student, but excelled in sport. Not surprisingly, his two best subjects were history and French.

He was happy at Cheam and became a proper little English schoolboy in no time at all. He lost the American accent he had gained at The Elms, and quickly became a member of the cricket team. It was unfortunate for him that when his parents finally parted, there was something of a tug-of-war over whether the German or the English relations should have responsibility for him.

Prince Andrew and Philip's four sisters felt he should be brought up in Germany. As sisters they felt they had prior claim. Princess Alice and her two brothers were convinced that Britian was the better environment.

For a while the German faction won. Philip's sister Theodora's husband, Berthold, the Margrave of Baden, had become the headmaster of the famous German school, Salem. The school had been founded by Dr Kurt Hahn, who believed in an education that encouraged physical fitness and self-reliance. It was not a system that produced intellectuals and the emphasis was on forcing a boy to face his own weaknesses and find more in himself. The idea was to create an aristocracy of accomplishment.

The school was flourishing when Hitler came to power in 1933 and immediately the Nazi regime turned their suspicious eyes on its methods and its headmaster. Hahn was a Jew, and Jews could not be permitted to influence the youth of Germany. It took only three months of Hitler's regime and Hahn was in prison.

It was fortunate that he had powerful friends all over Europe. Hitler was given no peace from these believers in Hahn's educational methods. He was released and permitted to emigrate to Britain.

Philip's brother-in-law, the Margrave, was appointed headmaster in his place, and it is ironic that as Hahn was travelling to Britain, where he was to create Gordonstoun, Philip was bound for Germany and Salem School.

Hitler's regime had already led to the departure of many foreign pupils from Salem and Berthold von Baden suggested that it would be a good idea to bring Philip to the school. It would be good publicity if a Prince was seen to leave the English school system for a German one. And also his sisters and his German relatives were closer than the British uncles. His heritage and background was German. He should be educated in Germany.

Reluctantly his mother agreed. Equally reluctantly the 12-year-old Philip left Cheam and was sent to the threatening atmosphere of Nazi Germany.

It was a mistake. The school was suffering from Nazi interference. Some teachers were pro-Nazi, some were not. Those who were, denounced those who were not. Boys were leaving, and two of the school's four houses had to be shut. Since it was a school where the progressive elite sent their children, the Nazi presence was unwelcome. Von Baden had decided that he would rather shut down the school than agree to the official demands for total nazification of all lessons, staff and pupils.

Threatened with prison if he did shut the school, the Margrave continued to struggle to keep the school going in Hahn's tradition. With the older boys and the younger teachers joining the S.S. storm troopers, and with the younger boys obliged to join the Hitler Youth, he had little chance of succeeding.

And he had another problem. As a foreigner, Prince Philip was exempt from joining any of these Nazi organizations, but he was not exempt from what he called the 'ghastly footslogging'. He thought the Nazis ridiculous and the Nazi salute hilarious. The upraised hand to him after his time as a Cheam schoolboy meant permission to leave the room! He made mock of the salute, mimicked the brown-shirt's goose-step and was generally dangerously irreverent and derisory.

Abruptly von Baden decided it would be better for Philip and better for him if the boy was sent back to England. There was an alternative—the new school which Hahn had opened in Scotland, Gordonstoun.

Certainly it was a wise move. The Prince loathed Salem, and years later wrote remembering one of the senior boys who had been responsible for the juniors: 'He so displeased the thugs that they caught him . . . and shaved his head. I lent him my Cheam 2nd XI cricket cap and I hope he has got it still.'

At Gordonstoun he was happy again, thriving under a regime which puts more importance on self-reliance and fitness than academic qualifications. Later, Philip was to say that he was 'one of those ignorant bums who never went to university—and a fat lot of harm it did me!' One could argue he had little need of university. He did have a few other advantages.

29

His training under Hahn has stuck. He is the archetypal Hahn disciple. He sent his sons there and persuaded Helene Cordet to send her son there. He has spent his life preaching the gospel of Hahn's methods. The Duke of Edinburgh's Award Scheme was Hahn's idea, and when Prince Philip told us all that we must get our fingers out, in one of his more controversial speeches, he was only punching home what he had learned at Gordonstoun.

His schooldays were happy. There was more building walls and manning coastguard stations than learning physics or reading philosophy. The curriculum, when it came to the academic, was more than somewhat lopsided in favour of the physical. But he liked Hahn and Hahn liked him, saying that 'his most marked trait was his undefeatable spirit'.

When the Prince left Gordonstoun to go to Dartmouth Royal Navy College for training in his chosen career, Hahn wrote of his royal pupil: 'His best is outstanding; his second best is not good enough. Prince Philip will make his mark in any profession where he will have to prove himself in a full trial of strength.'

Perhaps that trial of strength has been fought all these years in an effort to keep his own identity in a role that has no substance.

There was some contact with his own parents in the Gordonstoun years. He visited Athens for the first time at the age of 15 for a somewhat macabre reason. After a plebiscite, the Greek monarchy were returned yet again to the throne in 1935, and Philip's Greek Uncle George, after eleven years languishing in exile in London, was returned to the throne.

In those eleven years of Republican rule King Constantine I, Queen Sophie and George I's widow, Queen Olga, had all died and their mortal remains were buried in Florence. George II decided that they should all be brought home. They were to be reburied in the family crypt after lying in state for six days at Athens Cathedral. The whole occasion was to be a great ceremony of state.

He invited his relations, the crowned, and uncrowned heads of Europe to come to the ceremony and put them up at the luxurious Hotel Grande Bretagne in Athens.

Philip too asked for special leave from Gordonstoun and went off to buy himself his first formal clothes he had ever owned,

30

including a silk top hat. The hat was to have an unfortunate ending. On the day of the funeral, after a lobster dinner the night before, Philip felt decidedly queasy.

In the cathedral, while he watched his father form the guard of honour with his brothers and the archbishops assemble, he whispered desperately to his cousin Alexandra: 'I'm going to be sick.'

Somehow he kept control during the service, but in the procession back to the palace, the hat came in extremely handy! His problem was then what to do with it. Alighting from the car he thrust it into the hand of an unwilling aide.

More important was that in Athens he saw his mother and father again. His mother was not well enough to attend the ceremony, but he was able to spend time with her in her small house which she shared with a woman companion, Madame Socopol. There they pored together over old family photographs and he learned more of the history of the Battenbergs and the Glücksburgs.

He returned to Greece not long after for the wedding of his Uncle, Prince Paul, to a German princess, Frederika, who was destined to become the Queen of Greece and cause such political problems that she would be exiled with her husband. Philip received two requests from his parents on these visits. His mother asked if he would come and live with her, and his father pressed on him the idea of joining the Greek navy. Philip had already made up his mind to live as an Englishman, and if he joined the navy it would be that of his English uncles, the British Navy.

He made it clear, as gently as possible, that the answer to both requests was no.

It was in this period that two tragedies marred his happy life. His sister, Cecile, her husband and their two children were all killed in an aircrash. They were flying to England for the wedding of Prince Louis of Hesse to an English girl, the Honorable Margaret Geddes. Over Ostend, in a thick fog, their plane hit a factory chimney.

The second tragedy was perhaps even more personal and harder to bear. Uncle George, the Marquis of Milford Haven, died of cancer in the Autumn of 1938. He was only 46, and the young Prince had loved him as a surrogate father since he was 8 years old.

It was now that Lord Mountbatten came into the picture. He took over the responsibility for the 17-year-old Prince and Philip responded eagerly to this glamorous uncle. At that time Philip hero-worshipped his Uncle Dickie, and not without reason. He was an extraordinarily brilliant man, living a sophisticated life. His wife was rich and clever and they lived in an elegant home that sported a swift lift to the top floor and boasted a dressing room decorated as a replica of a ship's cabin. Heady stuff for a 17-year-old.

Uncle Dickie took over his responsibilities with the gusto that he put into everything. He used his influence to make sure young Philip took the entrance examination for Dartmouth and arranged a crammer course to fill the gaps in Hahn's system of education—it is fair to say the Prince Philip's spelling was appalling for one so expensively educated. He organized his nephew's life, and he began to wonder if perhaps, just perhaps, it would be possible to marry this sprig of the Mountbatten tree to the future Queen of England.

And decided it was worth a try.

3

THE PLOT

Considering the enormous differences in their temperaments, the marriage between the Queen and Prince Philip has worked remarkably well. But it was not entirely a marriage made in heaven. There were other factors. Ambition and self-interest were as involved as Cupid and true love. While the Queen was still in the nursery Philip's elders were plotting and planning. To be the consort of the future Queen was a glittering prize and there were those, not Philip himself, who worked for this marriage of considerable convenience—for the groom and his relations.

The plan to marry Philip to Lilibet had began as early as the summer of 1939, when the Queen was just 13 and Prince Philip 18. Vice-Admiral Harold Tom Baillie-Grohman was captain of the battleship *Ramillies* in the Mediterranean Fleet when he received an unexpected cable from Lord Louis Mountbatten. It was a request for him to take Mountbatten's nephew, Prince Philip of Greece, into his ship.

Baillie-Grohman instantly agreed. He had served both with Lord Mountbatten, who was very much of the Naval Establishment, and Mountbatten's father (Philip's grandfather) Admiral Prince Louis of Battenberg (afterwards Marquis of Milford Haven). Battenberg, who was of German descent, had been the British Navy's first Sea Lord in World War I until anti-German feeling drove him to resign.

Therefore, Midshipman Philip Mountbatten, Prince of Greece, fresh out of Dartmouth Royal Naval College, duly reported for duty. It was his first naval posting since finishing his cadetship, after romping home with the book-token prize for being the best student of the year. He swopped the book-token for a book on the defence of Britain which would seem to indicate where his loyalties lay.

The 18-year-old prince was, wrote Baillie-Grohman in his unpublished memoirs, a particularly handsome young fellow, attractive in all his ways. He was also eager and hardworking.

The captain of the *Ramillies* had a yarn with Philip soon after he arrived aboard, as he did with all new officers. He remembered well the talk with Philip, for it took and expected turn.

Baillie-Grohman pointed out that as a foreign subject, the young Philip would only be able to reach the rank of Acting Sub-Lieutenant in the Royal Navy. To get further he would have to become naturalized. Did he want to go on in the Navy? Baillie-Grohman asked, and received an emphatic 'yes'.

Then came the breathtaker when Philip went on to say:

'My Uncle Dickie has ideas for me; he thinks I could marry Princess Elizabeth.'

The captain was somewhat taken aback, and after some hesitation asked: 'Are you really fond of her?'

'Oh, yes, very,' said Philip. 'I write to her every week.'

Baillie-Grohman, after thinking what an entirely suitable partner his new midshipman was likely to make for the Princess, immediately wrote the conversation down, so he could be sure that his memory would not be at fault in the future.

He also strongly advised the young Greek Prince not to mention the matter of Princess Elizabeth to anyone else aboard. He was aware that some of the more ambitious officers of the *Ramillies* would have been very busy trying to obtain a future foothold in the Palace should they have discovered that their fellow officer was a possible consort to the next Queen. On the whole, Baillie-Grohman felt he could have done without this gratuitous bit of information.

Therefore, he says stoutly, he was very careful to treat Prince Philip in exactly the same way as his other officers. Not only because Uncle Dickie had particularly asked that he should do this, but because to show any favouritism could make Philip's life difficult in the gun room.

But at that moment, in spite of Uncle Dickie's plans for a glittering future, Prince Philip was more concerned with his career. For one thing, the Princess Elizabeth, aged 13, was hardly ripe for marriage and would not be for some years. Philip, at 18, was not thinking of marriage either. He was a first-class seaman and eager to be on active duty in order to advance his career—an urgent need for a young man with no money or home of his own.

As Baillie-Grohman had pointed out, it was necessary for him to become a British subject. Quite apart from being unable to wed the heir presumptive without being naturalized, he couldn't take a permanent commission in the British navy, either.

His difficulty was that he was a thorny problem to the Admiralty and the Home Office who, since Mountbatten was his uncle, could not just ignore him. By the autumn of 1939 Germany was at war with Britain, but Germany was not at war with Greece. Philip was a citizen of a neutral power. He had requested to be naturalized time and time again, but there were diplomatic problems involved.

Uncle Dickie Mountbatten again came to the rescue, pulling strings until the Admiralty gave permission for Prince Philip of Greece to carry on his naval career. Even before Philip became a British subject in 1947 the rules were bent sufficiently for him to become a First Lieutenant. Baillie-Grohman's dire warnings of checkmate at Acting Sub-Lieutenant were ignored. Perhaps because it was wartime, perhaps because of Uncle Dickie's influence—but certainly because the young prince richly deserved the promotions that he was given.

Bending the rules was one thing, but nobody quite knew what to do about Philip diplomatically. Ordinary aliens could change nationality easily. But this was a prince of a neutral country. For the time being he had to remain Midshipman Prince Philip of Greece.

The *Ramillies* was to escort troop convoys from Australia to Egypt, which gave Philip his first trip to a country that he would visit in a very different style and role many years on. And his first visit was not brief. There were to be a few week's refitting for the *Ramillies* after the first escort duty to Egypt was finished. Baillie-Grohman, with his not-so-welcome special knowledge of Philip's possible future was uneasy about the effect that the handsome young officer would have on the Sydney girls. He feared the worst, and the worst could bring possible repercussions. He may have blanched at the thought of the coals of fire that would be heaped on his head by his old friend Dickie Mountbatten should young Philip stray out of line and spoil his chances with the British royal family. Baillie-Grohman, having served with Mountbatten, was undoubtedly aware that if Uncle Dickie had ideas, those ideas had a very good chance of reaching fruition. He, Baillie-Grohman, would not be popular if any action of his interrupted the germination stage.

Therefore, when the *Ramillies* was refuelling at Freemantle, Baillie-Grohman prudently phoned an old friend, Hunter Patterson, who owned a fine sheep station about 500 miles from Sydney. Would he and his wife take a few parties of young officers, he asked, while the refit was taking place?

Happily, Hunter Patterson agreed. Prince Philip, who had been accepting hospitality all his life, was keen to go, and with his fare paid by Mr Patterson, set off for the sheep station at Deniliquin safe from the temptations of the fleshpots of Sydney.

Lord Mountbatten, had he known it, could sleep easy in his bunk.

But Lord Mountbatten was not Philip's only champion. There were others who believed he could become consort to the future British Queen.

It was just about a year later—21 January 1941—when the Tory MP, Sir Henry 'Chips' Channon, was in the Balkans on a wartime mission that took him to neutral Greece. Chips Channon, an enormously wealthy, sexually uncertain snob with a taste for titles, recorded his impressions of Prince Philip's immediate family.

'There is the isolated King who sees no-one; there are the Crown Prince [today the exiled King] and Princess (Frederika) who, madly in love, remain aloof from the world with their babies and their passion. (She is a touch unpopular, being German. I met her first dining with General Goering in 1936): there is Princess Andrew [Prince Philip's mother] who is eccentric to say the least and lives in semi-retirement: there is Prince Andrew [Prince Philip's father] who philanders on the Riviera whilst his son Prince Philip is serving in our navy . . .'

The King, George II, had already been dispossessed of his throne once. And with war imminent, prospects for an unpopular Royal family did not look good.

Chips Channon, father of Paul Channon, whose daughter Olivia died so tragically of a drug overdose in 1986, was invited to a cocktail party at an Athen's home. He, like Baillie-Grohman, recorded the event in his diary. He wrote:

'An enjoyable Greek cocktail party. Prince Philip of Greece was there. He is extraordinarily handsome . . . He is to be our Prince Consort, and that is why he is serving in our Navy. He is charming, but I deplore such a marriage. He and Princess Elizabeth are too interrelated.'

His information came from a conversation with Princess Nicholas of Greece, the mother of Marina, Duchess of Kent. Marina, who had married our King George VI's younger brother was a Greek princess. Her husband, a serving RAF officer, was killed in the war. Philip was her second cousin, and after the war, when Philip was seriously courting the young Princess Elizabeth, Marina's Buckinghamshire home, Coppins, was to be a very convenient 'safe house' where the young couple could meet without drawing unwelcome attention to themselves.

That was far into the future. But by 1941, with Princess Elizabeth still a white-socked schoolgirl, the crowned heads of Europe, desperately clinging to their wobbly thrones, had their sights on the secure British throne, THE dynastic prize, for at least one of their dispossessed members.

Prince Philip of Greece, sixth in line to the Greek throne, could only be a consort in Britain, true. But historically another foreign royal, the German Prince Albert, hadn't done too badly out of being Number Two at Buckingham Palace. The European crowned heads of the forties were almost entirely descended from Albert and Queen Victoria (indeed, still are). Therefore, they chose to forget that, in spite of Victoria's unwavering love for him, Prince Albert was never fully accepted by the British people. Just as today, many of the British still harbour faint, and possibly equally unjust, doubts about Queen Elizabeth II's consort.

Foreign royalty saw such an advantageous marriage as a

possibility and received backing from their members in England — Queen Mary, born a German Princess and the Duchess of Kent.

Even when the Princess and Prince Philip had become secretly engaged, while the royal family were officially denying any such thing, there was a deliberately engineered disclosure by the foreign royals. The Greek royal newspaper, *Helleni-con Aema*, published that there was an impending announcement of the betrothal of Princess Elizabeth to Prince Philip of Greece.

In Britain, the rumours continued to be denied.

Mountbatten, was the most persistent of them. He wrote to King George VI from Southeast Asia where he was serving, urging that Prince Philip be helped to get his naturalization papers. The King replied testily that it was also a matter for the King of Greece who had just at that time fled his country and taken refuge in London with both his ministers and his country's gold reserves. And the King of Greece was torn in two directions. The desire to see one of his relatives snug in the shelter of the British monarchy was fighting against his hope that one day his throne would be restored to him. Because if it was, he would need all the family support he could get.

Whether or not Philip knew of these plots and plans, we do not know. What we do know, is that like most serving officers he was more concerned with the war and his career.

But George VI was not content with the prospect of Prince Philip as a son-in-law. Philip was not British, he had no solid background. Perhaps he knew more about the young man's private adventures than his still immature daughter did. And he was being heavily nudged by Mountbatten. The King, a man with a mind of his own, disliked being nudged.

And then there was an indiscreet conversation between King George of the Hellenes and the King — the Greek King alluding to a possible union between his kinsman and the Princess Elizabeth.

'It is a pity that Philip and Alexandra [Queen Alexandra of Yugoslavia] did not marry, but it might be for the best,' he said, adding 'It would be nice if we could reunite our families and our countries through Lilibet and Philip. It seems Lilibet is in love with Philip, and I know he adores her.'

An angry George VI, aware that others could be listening, said firmly that Philip need not think about it for the present. 'They are both too young,' he said flatly.

He was to say, but privately, that if Philip was ever to wed his daughter, he must first win the plaudits of the people and present himself as an Englishman. Naturalization, which would mean completely renouncing his rights to the Greek throne, was essential. The Queen went along with his views. She saw no reason why Elizabeth should not wait. She herself had made the King wait until she was absolutely sure of the rightness of the marriage. The most British of women, she would perhaps have preferred a British husband for her daughter. A child of World War I, she had little sympathy with Germany.

Even today she does not care for the family's German relatives —with the exception of 'Dear Peggy Hesse'. But then Peggy Hesse was the Honourable Margaret Geddes, who married a German Prince.

It was Lord Mountbatten who worked hardest for the marriage. He saw himself as a kingmaker, though some in court circles were more inclined to refer to him as a meddler. He was actively to encourage the relationship between the young Princess and the good-looking naval officer, fanning the flames of their mutual attraction. Having seen the possibilities, he was not a man to let them pass. Years later, he would say complacently: 'After all, who else could Lilibet have married? There weren't that many suitable Princes or other Royalty about.'

But Mountbatten had a vested interest in his nephew marrying the heir presumptive. He was brilliant, loyal and charming; a remarkable man, but when it came to birth and breeding he was also a colossal snob. He firmly believed that royalty should marry royalty—though he made an exception in his own case and married the richest woman in Britain, Edwina Ashley.

His own father, Prince Louis of Battenberg had been forced to drop his titles and his German name in World War I's anti-German hysteria. King George V, of German descent himself, hastily changed his name to Windsor, and then decreed that all

German princes living in Britain should drop their titles and take British names. Louis of Battenberg became the first Marquis of Milford Haven and the family name became Mountbatten. On his death, his eldest son took the Milford Haven title. His second son was Lord Louis Mountbatten, Philip's Uncle Dickie. But the family lost their right to call themselves HRH. This was always a source of burning resentment to Lord Mountbatten, though both his sisters got their royal style back. His sister, Louise, had married HRH the King of Sweden. His other sister, Philip's mother, married HRH Prince Andrew of Greece.

The family name, and perpetuating it, was of enormous importance to Lord Mountbatten. He felt himself to be royal. And when he came to write his own family tree, it was his Polish grandmother Fraulein Julie von Hauke, the daughter of a Russian general who received the least coverage. Perhaps because her great-grandfather had been a tradesman in Mainz. She was lady-in-waiting to the Tsarina and she married Prince Alexander of Hesse, the Tsarina's brother, in 1851 after a long passionate affair with him. He had married beneath his station and was immediately cashiered from the Russian Imperial Guard and stripped of his rank. He was no longer welcome at any of the courts of Europe.

Eventually a decree elevated Fraulein Julie von Hauke to the rank, dignity and title of Countess von Battenberg but her children would have no rights or claim to the succession to the throne.

In other words, any children of the union would bear the mother's new name—Battenberg—but be deprived of all princely titles. Thus the Battenbergs were born, the name chosen from a defunct Middle Ages title.

Lord Mountbatten keenly felt the deprivation of these princely titles. Marrying his nephew to the Queen of England, would redress the balance and also right the wrongs done to his father in World War I. Mountbatten was determined it would happen.

It did.

But plot and plan as he might, Lord Mountbatten had one unexpected stroke of good fortune in his campaign for honour and riches for his nephew. What he could not have foreseen was that Princess Elizabeth would fall in love with Prince Philip from their very first meeting.

And of this there is no doubt. Sir John Wheeler-Bennett who wrote the official biography of King George VI, said of Prince Philip of Greece: 'This was the man with whom Princess Elizabeth had been in love from their first meeting.'

The biography was scrutinized and approved by Queen Elizabeth. She never changed a word of that telling sentence.

Many years later, Mountbatten was to attempt to repeat his triumph. In the days when Princess Diana was still a plump schoolgirl, he connived the marriage of Prince Charles to his granddaughter, Amanda Knatchbull. This time he failed. But there are those who remain convinced that if Lady Diana Spencer had not so fortuitously appeared one day in 1980, we would one day have found ourselves with Britain's first Queen Amanda.

4

THE COURTSHIP

According to Baillie-Grohman's testimony, Lord Mountbatten's campaign to bring about a royal marriage had begun early. Could it have commenced one rainy summer's day in July 1939? Lord Mountbatten was then aide-de-camp to King George VI and the royal family were on holiday, cruising the south coast prior to visiting Balmoral, in *Britannia's* predecessor, the *Victoria and Albert*. For some reason the King had decided to sail the huge white-and-gold yacht with her painted figure-head up the River Dart for a weekend private visit to Dartmouth Royal Naval College.

It was at this prestigious establishment that the King, who always considered himself a sailor first and foremost, had rounded off his education in 1912. Dartmouth is a vast red-brick building set high on a hill above the river where boys are trained to be naval officers and as the yacht arrived the King and his family were greeted by 900 cheering would-be admirals. It was a rum sort of visit, considering that the shy King, though having quite enjoyed his stay there, had not done particularly well with the final examinations, coming embarrassingly near the bottom of the class. But, however, on 22 July 1939 the royal yacht arrived. On board were the King, the Queen and his two young daughters, Princess Elizabeth and Princess Margaret Rose.

Accompanying them—Uncle Dickie Mountbatten.

It comes as no surprise to find that the Dartmouth college was housing a very new cadet; Mountbatten's 18 year old nephew, Prince Philip. Lord Mountbatten had arranged for his nephew to take an examination as a special-entry public schoolboy cadet and Philip had passed with no difficulty at all. Later he was to say that left to his own devices he would have gone into the RAF, but Uncle Dickie was keen to carry on the Battenberg/Mountbatten naval tradition.

The King had planned to attend morning service in the college chapel but unfortunately a good many of the younger cadets had come down with mumps. Measles was also about. Owing to the risk of infection, it was decided that the little Princesses should not go. They took shelter instead at the home of Captain Dalrymple-Hamilton, the officer in charge of college. He had two slightly older children, and there was a model railway laid out on the nursery floor.

Fortuitously, Uncle Dickie's handsome blond nephew had been struck by neither measles nor mumps. Uncle Dickie had him hauled out of matins to entertain the little girls. Philip, according to his biographer cousin, Queen Alexandra of Yugoslavia, was not too enthusiastic about looking after a girl of 13 and another of 9. But he took his orders and did his duty manfully.

The three youngsters ate ginger crackers and drank lemonade. they played for a while with the train-set, kneeling on the floor, watched by their governess, Marion Crawford. Then the ever-restless Prince suggested a game of croquet. They played and after he had won the game, as boys do, young Philip began to show off. He entertained the little girls by leaping over a tennis net. Having won prizes at Gordonstoun for the high jump, he did this rather well.

He much impressed the 13-year-old little Lilibet. She said to her governess, 'How good he is Crawfie—how high he can jump!'

He was to jump a great deal higher.

Even for that period, the two young Princesses were sheltered and unsophisticated. Prince Philip, on the other hand, was a much-travelled cosmopolitan, already forceful and sure of himself. His circumstances, his skill at finding someone to give him a roof, had made him a confident survivor. But perhaps his biggest asset at 18 was that he had been blessed with remarkably good looks. He was extremely handsome, tall and thin but without being gangly. He had a lot of yellow hair and his eyes were very blue. He looked like an ancient Greek or a viking. Not surprisingly, the unworldly Princess Elizabeth was deeply impressed, but shy in his presence. She watched his every move, fascinated, but said little.

As the heir to the throne, she had duties to perform that day. She planted a tree, and the King and his family inspected the college grounds and the pool. All the cadet captains were asked to dinner on the yacht that night, but Lilibet, still a member of the nursery, had gone to bed.

Not to be beaten, Uncle Dickie managed to procure an invitation for Philip to lunch on the yacht. 'Crawfie' records that he found it easier to relate to the younger, but more extrovert Princess Margaret. He spent the afternoon laughing a lot and teasing her. Margaret's big sister seems to have worried more about him eating a good tea. Again she said little but watched pink cheeked and admiring while he consumed an enormous plate of prawns and a banana split.

Even today, according to Philip's cousin, Queen Alexandra, he teases the Queen about her shyness on that meeting. It is surprisingly, the first that they can both remember, though there had been other occasions when they had been at the same royal gatherings. Both had attended Princess Marina's wedding to the Duke of Kent in 1934 and the Prince had been a guest at Elizabeth's father's coronation in 1937.

The day following the prawn tea, the royal yacht sailed away. Crawfie records: 'We all said good-bye, and the engines started. It is a tricky business getting out of Dartmouth harbour. Sir Dudley North was the Captain in charge. Finally we got well out into the Channel. All the boys from Dartmouth had been allowed to get any sort of craft they could find—motor boats, rowing boats, and so on—and they followed the *Victoria and Albert* quite a long way. Then the King got very alarmed and said to Sir Dudley North, "It's ridiculous and most unsafe. You must signal them to go back."

'Most of the boys did go back immediately, and all the others followed shortly except this one solitary figure whom we saw rowing away as hard as he could, who was, of course, Philip. Lilibet took the glasses and had a long look at him. In the end the King said, "The young fool. He must go back, otherwise we will have to heave to and send him back."

'At last Philip seemed to realise they did want him to go back—they were shouting at him through the megaphone—and he turned back while we gazed at him until he became just a very small speck in the distance.'

According to her governess, Elizabeth had caught a disease more dangerous than mumps; she had an advanced case of puppy love. It is not surprising that the heir presumptive, watching all this boyish daring-do through enormous binoculars, did not forget the blond Viking prince.

But just how and when the courtship really began is uncertain. Who wrote first to whom? But a correspondence did begin, and if the Vice-Admiral is to be believed—and why should one not believe him—letters had been exchanged as early as 1939, perhaps soon after that first meeting.

Certainly Uncle Dickie fixed up a theatre party with the King, the Queen and Prince Philip to see *Sunny Side Up* while the young midshipman was on leave before joining *Ramillies*. But there was no further opportunity to meet the Princess. Almost immediately afterwards Philip left for Colombo to join his ship. His stay with Baillie-Grohman was short. Early in 1940 he was transferred to HMS *Kent*, where with his in-built ability to get on in most situations, he rapidly became popular—in spite of the disadvantage of being a foreign Prince!

As midshipman, he was required to fill in daily the Admiralty Form S.519. He had to record in his own language anything interesting or important that happened. Rather pompously the Admiralty explained: 'The objects of keeping the journal are to train Midshipmen in (a) the power of observation, (b) the power of expression, (c) the habit of orderliness.'

Philip crossed out 'Mr' at the top of the form and put in its place Philip, Prince of Greece.

The *Kent* put in at Durban where the local girls gave the crew a warm welcome. Form S.519 as recorded by Philip, Prince of Greece, remarks that: 'The fact that many hearts were left behind in Durban is not surprising.' And other recorded short leaves spent in the same town are usually honoured by an exclamation mark in the journal.

On Philip's nineteenth birthday, 10 June 1940, Mussolini declared war on Greece. This action changed Prince Philip's career prospects completely. And by October, when Greece had become one of the allies, he was no longer a Prince of a neutral power. As a neutral it would have been a great embarrassment to the British Government should someone have dropped a bomb on him or seen him off the scene in some fashion while on active duty. As an ally it was not such a serious matter—at least to the British. He was now entitled to be on our side. Uncle Dickie, anxious to further his nephew's career, wrote many letters reminding the Naval powers-that-be and the Establishment of this. And though the British Government still hesitated to naturalize the Prince, in January 1941 he was at least sent to the war zone.

The Admirality transferred him to HMS *Valiant* which was seeing active service in the Mediterranean. And before he went, he spent a brief leave in Uncle Dickie's home at 16 Chester Street, where he saw old friends, including Helene Cordet. With this new posting, he was nearer both to Greece, his Greek relatives and his Uncle Dickie who was then commanding a destroyer flotilla.

But were he and the Princess corresponding at this time or not? Prince Philip certainly sent the Princess a Christmas card in 1940. She was dismayed to find that he was not on the family Christmas-card list. Long into the new year she was pestering her father to send a return card.

If she truly had fallen in love with him, the years that followed brought her little contact with him. It was not until the war ended and he returned to Britain from overseas service that she had any opportunity to know him properly.

Whether or not Philip had marriage to her on his mind as so many of his relatives did, we do not know. What we do know, is that like most serving officers when he was not fighting hard, he was playing hard.

He had barely joined the battleship *Valiant* when she was engaged in bombarding the Libyan coast and then a few days later he was caught up in a decidedly hairy sea battle south of Sicily. The young Philip, in charge of a section of searchlight control acquitted himself well under heavy bombing from enemy aircraft and had earned the leave he was given after the battle. He went to Greece and was able to visit his mother in Athens and see his other royal relatives, including his childhood friend, Princess Alexandra of Greece. He found time for a lot of partying. He showed off a little about his first bit of active service and the five bombs that had narrowly missed the *Valiant*. And why not? He was only 19.

By the time he was back as sea, the war was hotting up. Greece was invaded and his Greek relatives were forced to leave Athens for Crete. Crete, too, was to fall to the Germans, and the Greek royal family were again on the move, this time to Egypt.

On 28 March 1941, Philip fought at the Battle of Matapan, and six months later he was mentioned in dispatches for his services manning the searchlights in HMS *Valiant* during the battle off the Greek mainland's most southerly cape. His commander, Admiral Sir Charles Morgan, reported: 'Thanks to his alertness and appreciation of the situation, we were able to sink in five minutes two eight-inch-gun Italian crusiers.'

He had helped to win a great victory. The Italians lost two destroyers, three cruisers and all hope of retaining control of the sea in that area.

King George II of the Helenes also awarded his cousin with a medal, the Greek War Cross of Valour.

Little more than a month later, in May, Lord Mountbatten's ship, HMS *Kelly* was sunk by a direct hit from a 1,000lb bomb. The *Kelly* turned turtle. Altogether, 210 seamen died on her and HMS *Kashmir*, which was also sunk. But Lord Mountbatten bobbed up again, rescued by the destroyer *Kipling* and was ferried to Alexandria where the Greek royal family had taken refuge and where his nephew was taking a spot of leave.

The first person ashore, whom Mountbatten saw was a cheery young midshipman, grinning all over his face. It was Philip.

'You've no idea how funny you look,' he told his uncle unfeelingly. 'Your face is absolutely brown and your eyes are bright red.'

But Mountbatten had survived to appear urbane and beautifully turned out in naval whites to visit his royal relations in

47

Alexandria. Queen Alexandra recalls that he was furious at the loss of a set of gold-backed hair brushes, gone forever to the bottom with the ill-fated *Kelly*,.

Like his Uncle, Philip, too, kept bobbing up.

More leave led to more meetings with his cousin Alexandra in Alexandria, Cairo and even Cape Town where some of the Greek royals were sheltering at Groote Schuur, General Smut's official home. This meeting came about when he left the *Valiant* to return to Britain to take his sub-lieutenant's examination. He had been sent from Port Said on the *Duchess of Athol*, an old liner, doing duty as a troopship. She was taking the safer Cape route back to England.

At Cape Town, Philip and four other midshipman talked themselves on to a faster, newer ship which was to pick up Canadian troops in Nova Scotia. Back home in Britain, he spent a rare leave in the October at Windsor Castle. Princess Elizabeth was still, at 15, in the schoolroom. Philip spent his time entertaining the King, and the King remarked in his diary how the young officer had amused him with tales of his adventures in the Mediterranean. It was at this time that the Prince took his sub-lieutenant's examination and passed with ease. In February 1942 his promotion to Sub-Lieutenant was confirmed and he was posted to HMS *Wallace* in Rosyth on the Firth of Forth, Scotland. He was to stay there until July 1943.

Now his courtship of the young Princess could really begin. The Princess sent him a Christmas card and enclosed a photograph of herself with it. He sent her one back—the only one he had, taken when he was a sub-lieutenant, before he gained his promotion. On his return from the Cape he was invited to Windsor, formally, and there was little time for the young couple to be alone. There were other occasional meetings—they danced together for the first time at a small private dance given by the beautiful Marina, Duchess of Kent at her Ivor home, Coppins. And he would occasionally be invited for a Windsor weekend.

Not that he had much leave. The new posting to Scotland was no picnic. The *Wallace* was on convoy duty along what was known as E-boat Alley—from Rosyth down the east coast to Grimsby and Sheerness. The job was an extremely dangerous one. The trips took about two-and-a-half days in each direction. Convoys were made up of as many as a hundred merchant ships which meant that two destroyers had to guard twenty miles of slow moving vessels. There were air attacks, E-boat attacks and mines to contend with as well as the dreadful weather of the North Sea. But it all gave the Prince the opportunity to show his mettle. It only took until October 1942 for him to be promoted to Sub-Lieutenant. He was aged 21, and the youngest man in the Royal Navy to hold this rank.

Every unmarried Wren on the Rosyth base had her sights set on him, but Prince Philip never became involved with any of them. Those who worked with him at that time could not believe that such an attractive man did not have a girl somewhere, but he did not invite questions.

If his companions began to discuss personal relationships, he held back from the conversation. He gave out an aura of being different, and special. And he expected to be treated as if he was.

But he had made one close friend; another young First Lieutenant, Michael Parker, a good-looking, lively Australian who was commanding HMS *Lauderdale*. They had both passed their First Lieutenant's exams at much at the same time; their ships were both new *Hunt*-class destroyers and both wanted his ship to be the best in the flotilla. The rivalry between them was intense, but they were too alike, had too much in common, not to become friends.

With his Australian background, Michael Parker was not particularly impressed with Philip's title. Before he introduced his friend to his young fiancée Eileen, he said 'I've told you about him, remember? He's called Philip of Greece. Some sort of Greek prince. I feel sure you'll like him.'

At that first meeting, the future Mrs Parker records in her book *Step Aside for Royalty*, what a handsome man Prince Philip was. She describes him as tall with piercing blue eyes and a shock of blond hair swept back from his forehead.

'When Prince Philip came into the wardroom that Saturday afternoon, I was seated at a table, preoccupied with darning some of Mike's socks. He (Prince Philip) joked that he had plenty of his own socks suffering from "shell-shock". I replied that if he could be bothered to bring them over (*Lauderdale* and *Wallace* were often berthed next to each other) I would be glad to oblige.

' "What I can't understand about darning," he mused, "is where the wool goes if there is a hole in the sock."

'When I offered to darn his socks, nobody, not even Mike had any idea that they were being knitted for him by the future Queen of England.'

But the Princess, never good at knitting or needlecrafts, might have been slaving over the handsome lieutenant's socks, but he on his leaves to London was busy breaking hearts.

Princess Alexandra says that the charm of Prince Philip had spread, like influenza in London. She recognized the symptoms when her girl friends gushed about his charm, his Viking looks, and wanted to know where he was. She spent one afternoon at the tailors with the Prince, expecting to be asked to tea. Not a bit of it. Suddenly he had to dash off.

'Who is it?' she challenged, listing his admirers.

He never said, but he did blush.

'Fond mothers would "fairy godmother" him for all they were worth,' Alexandra records in her book, *Prince Philip, A Family Portrait*. 'When Philip had a severe bout of 'flu it was no surprise to find him recovering in a suite in Claridges belonging to a hospitable family who had shown Philip a great deal of kindness. I sat by his bed and reproached him for not seeing enough of Mummy and myself, while he cheerfully plucked the grapes somebody else had sent him and ejected the pips at me with blithe, naval accuracy.

But when Alexandra and her future husband, King Peter, made a visit to Windsor to take tea with the royal family, Prince Philip's name was never mentioned.

It was in 1943 when things began to move. In July HMS *Wallace* left Scarpa Flow for the Mediterranean for a brief period. She was to patrol, while American airborne troops and British paratroopers descended on Italy.

On their return, in November, the *Wallace* went in dock for a refit that eventually took eight months. Philip was free to bring himself to London, where he lived in the attic of Mountbatten's Belgravia home, sleeping on a camp bed. He had the house to himself. Lord Mountbatten was in command of military operations in Southeast Asia and Lady Mountbatten was working for the Red Cross and St John's Ambulance Brigade.

Because he had nowhere else much to go, as he put it, he was invited to spent Christmas with the royal family at Windsor.

Crawfie recorded the occasion.

'Philip appeared on the scene again. It was quite a time since we had seen him. We were all involved in one of the pantomimes [a Christmas tradition at Windsor], very excited just before our first performance, when Lilibet came to me, looking rather pink. "Who do you think is coming to see us act, Crawfie? Philip".

'He had been in the Navy for some time and I wondered what he would be like now he was grown-up. He was, I knew, to sit in the front row, and I took a moment off to have a look at him.

'He was greatly changed. It was a grave and charming young man who sat there, with nothing of the rather bumptious boy I had first known about him now. He looked more than ever, I thought, like a Viking, weather-beaten and strained, and his manners left nothing to be desired.'

Lilibet acted better than she had ever done before; she was animated, there was a sparkle about her.

She was nearly 18 and in love.

Come August 1944 Philip went far away again. He was posted, with Uncle Dickie's blessing, to HMS *Whelp*, a ship of the 27th Destroyer Fleet, engaged against the Japanese in the Pacific. Usefully, Uncle Dickie was Supreme Allied Commander in Southeast Asia. Philip's mate, Michael Parker, was posted to another destroyer in the flotilla, HMS *Wessex*. And Uncle Dickie had actively begun his campaign for his nephew's marriage to Princess Elizabeth.

By now Prince Philip was corresponding quite openly with the Princess. It was common-knowledge on the *Whelp* that he was courting the future Queen. Their letters to each other came and went with the rest of the crew's mail. Nor did Philip object when the lower deck shouted: 'There's Jimmy-the-one's party!' when they saw newsreels of the Princess when *Whelp* was in harbour.

He and Michael managed some shore leave in Australia, and Michael introduced the Prince to his family. It was at the period when the Prince was sporting his large, blond beard. Michael

Parker had shaved his off, and when inevitably, reporters caught up with Philip, he would say: 'That's the man you want,' pointing at his fellow First Lieutenant, before disappearing into the crowd.

The two of them had a marvellous time. Though the Prince was already being pointed out as the man who was to marry Princess Elizabeth, he was able to enjoy himself at endless parties with an amazing variety of different girls on his arm. The Prince has always liked women and the company of women. On this Australian visit there were no shortages. He was pursued by an assortment of beautiful and mostly wealthy young women, but he was very, very cautious. There were no commitments, no involvements.

His cousin, Queen Alexandra, recalled that Philip no longer ignored gossip:

'Philip was no longer regardless of gossip. If awkward rumours arose he insisted firmly, sometimes rudely, that they should be scotched immediately. Once he returned from a ball to a friend's house with a young blonde in tow. They all sat and talked for a while and then it was noticed that Philip had quietly fallen asleep. It was getting rather late and the girl was obviously becoming concerned because her mother was waiting up for her. Rather than wake up an obviously tired-out lieutenant, the friend took the girl home. They had no sooner left the house than Philip opened an eye and smilingly offered his hostess, Mrs Judy Fallon, an explanation. He had noticed that heads were turning and nodding, in his direction, as they left the ball. If he had taken the girl home another hot rumour would have been in full flow.'

He had a great time, but never once did any situation get out of hand. Uncle Dickie would have been proud of him.

A year later on 6 August the Americans dropped the first atom bomb. Hiroshima was razed. Three days later Nagasaki met the same fate. The *Whelp*, with Philip aboard, joined the U.S. battle-ship *Missouri* in Tokyo Bay to receive the Japanese surrender. And the Prince, no doubt courtesy of Uncle Dickie, was aboard the *Missouri* when the surrender was signed. It was 2 September 1945 and ten days later, Lord Mountbatten accepted the surrender of the 730,000 Japanese in Southeast Asia in Singapore Town Hall.

The war was over.

The *Whelp* came home, bringing released prisoners of war with her, and since it seemed that Prince Philip would be posted to home waters, the Princess began to take matters into her own hands. Her father was still reluctant to think of her as grown-up. But she was 19 years old, and, though not as pretty as her younger sister, had a reserved, gentle charm and a radiant smile.

She was now free of the nursery and had been given her own footman, housemaid and, most important, her own drawing room. She placed a picture of Prince Philip on her own mantle-piece, and when the King protested that this was not very discreet, she exchanged it for one of the Prince, still in naval uniform but sporting the bushy blond beard he had grown in the South Pacific. Defiantly she insisted that the beard would put everyone off the scent. Needless to say, it did not.

Once he had returned to England, the Prince took to coming to Buckingham Palace so regularly that his visits became matter of course. He would drop in for an informal meal eaten in the old nursery, which was now Princess Margaret's sitting room. With Margaret ever present as an unwanted chaperone, they played silly games in the long corridors of the palace, games that were more suited to her age than theirs. Philip took the card that read 'nursery' off the door of Princess Margaret's sitting room and substituted one that said: 'Maggie's playroom'.

He telephoned Lilibet every evening, and like any other young girl in love she was restless and preoccupied until the phone rang. He also escorted her to theatres and parties. More privately, they walked hand in hand in Windsor Great Park. The press could not help but be alerted. Speculation began.

For a girl as unsophisticated and sensitive as the young Princess, the speculation was agony. Crawfie tells how one day Lilibet came back from visiting a factory. She was distressed.

'Crawfie, it was horrible!' she said. 'They shouted at me, "Where's Philip?" '

He had not yet proposed. She was not sure of his feelings. The shouts of the crowd must have reinforced all her own insecurities. Where, indeed, was Philip in this matter?

He was fighting his own romantic battles and when Judy Fallon joked that he had chosen the wrong girl—'Margaret is so much better looking'. Furious, Philip answered: 'You wouldn't say that if you knew them. Elizabeth is sweet and kind, just like her mother.'

There was also a defiance about his behaviour. He was certainly not making too much attempt to hide their closeness, no matter what the King thought. He wrote letters constantly to the Princess—and gave them to porters to post at the hotel where he was stationed. Happily, he was at least getting most weekends off. Lord Mountbatten's butler, John Dean was receiving very frequent phone calls from the Prince, looking for accommodation —as he had been all his life.

'Oh, John,' he would ask, 'has his Lordship gone away to Broadlands? Is it all right to have a bed for the night?'

Lord Mountbatten's staff seemed to have treated him like a small boy. Very often he came into the house by the area steps, and Mrs Cable, the cook, would shout: 'John, your boyfriend is here again, the old scoundrel.' Then as the future consort stood sheepishly by the kitchen table she would say: 'Well, you old tinker, I suppose you want a bed for the night! Are you hungry?'

He would protest he had eaten and didn't want to cause any trouble, but Mrs Cable liked to cook for him. In fact none of the staff minded doing anything for him. He was, they said, always considerate and undemanding.

On those weekends in London, either staying at Chester Street or the Milford Haven apartment in Kensington Palace, he would be out until the early hours. He was a member of the many nightclubs that wartime had spawned in London and he liked visiting them with his naval friends.

He would arrive at Chester Street for the weekend with a photograph of the Princess in a battered leather frame, but without a clean shirt or shoes. Overnight John Dean would wash and dry for him the ones he was wearing. He had hardly any civilian clothes at all and hardly any money, either.

None of these things troubled the Princess, though they may have weighed on her father's mind.

For the King still refused to accept that his adored daughter could have fallen in love with the first man she had met. He decided to put other men into her line of vision. There were dances, balls and dinners held at Windsor, Sandringham and Balmoral where various young aristocratic young gentlemen, mostly from the Guards' regiments, were paraded before and rejected by the Princess. Hugh Fitzroy, Earl of Euston, Charles Manners, Duke of Rutland, Lord Porchester and all British enough to satisfy the King's xenophobic nation. For the nation, the ordinary man in the street, was not enamoured with the idea of their Princess and future Queen marrying a Balkans Prince.

'Bloody bearded Greek!' the British working man said when the news broke of that picture on the Princess's mantlepiece.

It was not just the British working man that was uneasy at the thought. Many of the court, including Group Captain Peter Townsend, the King's Equerry and the man who one day would fall in love with Princess Margaret, were uncertain. The King asked the Special Branch to look into Prince Philip's background. Just in case. After all, his four sisters were all married to Germans, two of these husbands had fought against the British crown as officers in Hitler's forces.

Many at court also resented the Mountbatten connection. Was this marriage more evidence of his insatiable ambition? The very thought that one day, through his nephew, Lord Mountbatten could become the power behind the throne filled the Establishment with deep alarm.

Ordinary people asked why did the Princess have to marry someone Royal? The Queen herself was not royal born. The King had broken with custom when he married the daughter of an Earl. Most of the British people of the day could not see why their Princess should not marry a well-born Englishman.

The *Sunday Pictorial* ran a poll amongst its readers, asking whether or not they approved of the Princess marrying Philip. Forty per cent of the readers were against the marriage.

And the beard did not help at all.

Even the King said that if Philip was ever to wed his daughter, he must first win the plaudits of the people and present himself as an Englishman. Naturalization would mean completely re-nouncing his rights to the Greek throne—that was absolutely essential. He was well down in line to the Greek throne, but in the less settled climate of Eastern Europe he did have have some possibility of becoming a Greek king rather than a British consort. Time and history have proved Philip to have made the right choice. Time also proved that he has been able to win the respect, if not the hearts, of most of the people, most of the time.

Queen Mary, Elizabeth's grandmother, and staunchly on her side, could see exactly what her son, the King, was up to with all these parties and eligible young men. But since she had been born a German Princess herself, could see little wrong with a marriage between a Prince of Greece, whose father's Danish Royal family had already supplied three consorts to Kings and Queens of England (wives for James I and Edward VII, and a husband for Queen Anne). One of the things that enraged her about Hitler was that he spoke such terrible German!

Acidly she referred to the highly acceptable suitors that the King encouraged as the 'body guard'. And she confided to her lady-in-waiting, Lady Airlie, that the King and Queen wanted Elizabeth to meet more men, but she herself believed that her granddaughter was the sort of girl who fell in love for ever. 'She would always know her own mind,' she said. 'There is something very steadfast and determined in her.'

Prince Philip may not have known it, but he had a strong ally in Queen Mary. A member of the family was unwise enough to laugh at Prince Philip's schooling . . . 'in a crank school with theories of complete social equality where the boys were taught to mix with all and sundry.' Would such a background for the future Queen's consort prove useful or not?

'Useful,' said the dowager Queen shortly.

Queen Mary was convinced that her granddaughter had fallen in love with Philip on his first visit to Windsor that Christmas when Lilibet played the principal boy with such verve and sparkle. The old Queen liked Elizabeth's suitor very much. She described him as intelligent, with plenty of common sense, and very handsome with the attractive appearance of both the Glücksburgs and the Mountbattens. A bright, agreeable man was her verdict. She had met him early on when he first came to school in England at which time he often took tea with her at Buckingham Palace. She said then he was a nice little boy with very blue eyes. And when he joined the Royal Navy she added him to her knitting list of those relatives for whom she knitted scarves and gloves. She was also said to enjoy his naughty wardroom stories!

Philip also had an ally in George II of the Hellenes, though at that time he had more to worry about than who would become Elizabeth's future husband.

In 1944, when the Greek King finally did give his consent to the marriage, his nephew was a first-lieutenant, serving in HMS *Whelp* in Asian waters. Greece, freed from the Germans, was in the middle of a civil war. Winston Churchill and Anthony Eden managed to extract a sort of peace by visiting the country at Christmas, but the King was not permitted to return to his throne. Under the circumstances, the Home Office weren't too keen to grant naturalization to a member of the Greek royal family because it could appear that Britain was wholeheartedly shoring up the Greek royal cause. Alternatively, it could look as if things were so bad in the Hellenes that the Greek royals needed sanctuary in Britain.

Once again Philip's naturalization had to wait.

Come 1946, with the civil war over, Greece held a plebiscite to see whether or not the people wanted the monarchy back. The monarchy just scraped in. The King could go home again and back he went to Athens to reclaim his throne. Again Philip's attempts at naturalization were thwarted. This time the Foreign Office were concerned that it could be an embarrassment to the Greek royals to, so to speak, poach one of their member at the very moment the monarchy was restored.

The British Foreign Office refused naturalization for the umpteenth time and Philip had few to speak for him. The British King certainly wasn't pressing for anything to be done. In fact, the delay was something of a blessing for George VI who could not bear the idea of losing his daughter to another man.

The British Government, aware of the possibility of a union between the Prince and the Heir doubted the wisdom of such a marriage. The Greek royal family were accused of running a cruel and repressive regime. In Parliament a large group of socialist MPs condemned the Greek royals for 'barbaric atrocities'. Their tottering throne was kept upright only by the presence in the Hellenes of British troops who were fighting Russian-backed, left-wing troops.

But regardless of all these problems, it was in 1946 that the Prince took matters into his own hands and formally proposed to the Princess. He had been given a few week's leave from the navy to join the royal family at Balmoral for the summer holiday. He proposed by what the Queen is said to have described as 'some well-loved loch, the white clouds overhead and the curlews crying'.

And regardless of the rules, she disregarded her father, she ignored the wishes of the Government, and those of the Commonwealth (all of whom would have to agree the match) and accepted him then and there with all her heart. The diplomatic arguments held no sway against what she felt for Philip. She was determined to marry him, just as he was determined to marry her.

Faced with her acceptance, the thwarted King had to accept in principle that his daughter could become engaged. But under no circumstances was it to be announced. He insisted on absolute secrecy, and unfortunately for the young couple, he had a good reason to enforce the secrecy.

A trip to South Africa had long been arranged by the British royal family as a thank-you to the Dominion for joining the mother country in the war. It was to be a ten-week tour, and Princess Elizabeth's 21st birthday would be celebrated while they were away. It was planned that she should broadcast a speech of dedication to mark her coming-of-age. A fiancé on board would, in the King's view, have spoilt the whole thing, completely overshadowing the twenty-first birthday.

So, the couple would have to wait a little longer—almost a year from the time of the proposal in the early summer to the following May. The King was so determined on this that Buckingham Palace even gave a positive denial to the press that there was a royal engagement in the September of 1946.

But at least their intentions were openly before the royal

family. Their intimates knew the true situation even if the people were not to be told. They could meet whenever possible. Defiantly they let themselves be seen in public. Philip, now stationed in Corsham, Wiltshire at the training establishment known as HMS *Royal Arthur*, was in striking distance of London. It was a shore establishment where he was to instruct hard-nosed petty officers on naval warfare and current affairs. For an action man, it was not the happiest time of his life, but at least Corsham was not far from London. He had a black, green-upholstered, MG sports car, registration number HDK 99 and he would drive the ninety-eight-mile journey to London in an alarming one hour and forty minutes.

Crawfie remembers the car parked at the back entrance to Buckingham Palace and him rushing in as if not to waste a minute with the Princess. And when, in October 1946, Princess Elizabeth was bridesmaid at the wedding of Lord Mountbatten's elder daughter, Patricia, Prince Philip was also a guest and the King permitted him to be photographed with his daughter and himself. The picture was published everywhere—but with the King cropped out. And in her bridesmaid's dress it looked for all the world like a picture of a bride and groom, giving more confirmation to the anti-Mountbatten brigade that he was pushing for the wedding.

But there was to be no escape from another parting. Though Philip was now stationed in England, the Princess had no choice but to go to South Africa.

Two nights before the royal firm of four boarded HMS *Vanguard*, Lord Mountbatten gave a dinner party. The King and Queen, Prince Philip, Lord Milford Haven (Philip's boisterous cousin) and Lord and Lady Brabourne (Lord Mountbatten's son and daughter-in-law) were invited.

Mrs Cable cooked pheasant and the guests drank champagne. The King stayed with his own small decanter of Scotch. They ate in a small dining room dominated by a magnificent Franz Hals. Lord Mountbatten, soon off to become Viceroy of India, was in cracking form. The Prince and Princess were quiet and somewhat downhearted: the engagement was not announced. This was to be the last time that Prince Philip would see the Princess until her return from South Africa in three months' time. The King had decreed that it would not do at all for Philip to be seen seeing her off when they boarded the *Vanguard*.

Two days later, on 1 February, a desolate Princess, determined to do her duty as she had always done, set off for South Africa.

5

THE PLOT THICKENS

Dickie Mountbatten was not letting the grass grow under his feet. Well aware of the British antipathy to foreign royalty, he decided he must get the British newspapers on Philip's side. On 28 November 1946, Arthur Christiansen, editor of the *Daily Express*, John Gordon, editor of the *Sunday Express* and Mr E.J. Robertson, managing director of both papers were invited to Mountbatten's home in Chester Street for drinks. These were the two newspapers that, orchestrated by their proprietor, Lord Beaverbrook, had constantly fanned the British xenophobia in regard to the Mountbatten family. The Canadian Lord Beaverbrook could not abide the Mountbattens. He thought Lord Mountbatten opportunist and a meddler, and worse, blamed him for the terrible wartime defeat at Dieppe where 900 men, mostly Canadians, had been slaughtered and 2,000 taken prisoner. Mountbatten with Churchill had sanctioned the operation. And Mountbatten was convinced, with good reason, that the Express group were conducting a vendetta against him.

But here were three of Beaverbrook's most senior employees in Dickie's drawing room, chatting with Dickie's millionairess wife, while the lord, with all his considerable charm running over, poured drinks and most humbly asked their advice. What did they think about his nephew Philip becoming a British subject? What would the British public think about it? No word, of course, about the possible role of consort. Mountbatten was crossing one bridge at a time. But he did feel that it would be a good thing for his nephew to meet some of the newspaper 'big shots' as he described the three executives in his small living room. Otherwise they might snipe at the naturalization, particularly as the young man was his nephew.

So Philip was also there, self-effacing in the corner, carefully not drinking. With a couple of gin and tonics, the Beaverbrook press was disarmed. The two editors gave their opinion that because of his Prince Philip's war record and his blond looks, it ought to be all right. Happily, the chap did not look Greek at all, which was hardly surprising since Prince Philip has no Greek blood. Mountbatten waved his guests goodbye. The door shut behind them, he must have gleefully rubbed his hands, having guaranteed that both newspapers had had their teeth drawn. And indeed there were no protest or awkward questions when on 18 March 1947 Prince Philip was quietly granted naturalization. His name appeared along with more than 800 others in the *London Gazette*, mostly refugee Jews and Poles, all swearing allegiance to the British crown. There is some doubt as to whether he paid the registration fee of £10 (plus stamp duty) from his meagre savings, or whether the Home Office told him to forget it.

Lord Beaverbrook himself was said to be more astonished than angry that three tough, old newspaper men had been so easily disarmed, and it is not surprising that the matter did not rest there. The problems arising from Uncle Dickie's ploy came thirteen years later. His victory over Beaverbrook was to become a pyrrhic one. In the 9 August 1959 issue of the *Sunday Express*, John Gordon, now the paper's controversial columnist, was bleating that the Palace had denied that the Queen was pregnant, when she was all the time. He had a point. This is not an uncommon occurence even today. The Palace do not always tell the truth if it suits them not to do so.

John Gordon wrote: 'Some time before the Queen's engagement to Prince Philip was announced, I was told privately and definitely by one of her closest girl friends that Prince Philip was the man she would marry.

'I was assured they were deeply in love . . . When I sought confirmation at the Palace press office the reply was, "Nonsense".

'Shortly afterwards I was invited by Lord and Lady Mountbatten to call in at their home for drinks one evening, with two colleagues.

'We were introduced to Prince Philip who in fact handed around the drinks. A most likeable young man he is, and still remains.

'He told us frankly how deep was his affection for the Princess and hers for him. And that their engagement would be announced soon.

'Yet for weeks after that the Palace press office continued to deny emphatically that there was any foundation whatsoever for the suggestion of a marriage.

'An odd set-up, isn't it?'

Well, indeed it was. For such a conversation had not taken place. In public, Lord Mountbatten insisted that John Gordon's memory had 'played him false'. Privately he wrote to Prince Philip saying that he and Edwina were 'hopping mad with that bloody liar'.

John Gordon may have imagined, or lied, about the references to Princess Elizabeth, but he was right in that the Palace continued to deny the love affair right to the bitter end. Which is maybe why Prince Philip, three years later, was moved to call the *Daily Express* 'a bloody awful newspaper'.

For the purpose of becoming British, the Prince used Uncle Dickie's address, 16 Chester Street SW1. But events behind the scenes had not gone entirely smoothly. There was the question of which name Philip would choose. He now had to have a name. The days of grandly signing himself Philip and nothing more were over. The King suggested HRH Prince Philip—but at that time Philip was more interested in a naval rank than a title, and Chuter Ede, the socialist Home Secretary positively said that he must have a name—since the Greek royal family has no family name, he'd better decide on something.

Chuter Ede suggested going to the Royal College of Arms for proposals, and after long deliberations, the Heralds came up with the Duke of Oldcastle. This was an anglicized version of Oldenburg, the name of the German dukes who were the founders of the Danish royal family.

But even a socialist Home Secretary found Oldcastle too redolent of dark satanic mills (or even brown ale!) and the suggestion was rejected.

But Uncle Dickie, ever keen on getting his family name into prominence, was urging Mountbatten as having a fine ring to it, and pointing out that it sounded British enough for all that. Without a great deal of enthusiasm, probably aware of what Uncle Dickie was up to once again, Philip agreed. He became Lieutenant Philip Mountbatten, RN.

It is said that, understandably, he would have much preferred to use his father's real name, rather than his uncle's anglicized one. But it had to be admitted that Mountbatten had to be a great deal more acceptable to the xenophobic British than Schleswig-Holstein-Sönderburg-Glücksburg.

Uncle Dickie was delighted, just as he was to be eight years later when he was able to persuade the Queen that some of her descendents, notably the grandchildren of her younger sons, should be called Mountbatten-Windsor. Again it must be said, that this was not a move that had Prince Philip's blessing. The puzzle is why the Queen agreed. Could it have been a thank-you for Lord Mountbatten's support against the King in those days when she was so young and so much in love. Or more likely, simply to honour her husband?

The name is still not popular with the British Establishment. Years later, when Princess Anne married, the great question was which name to put on the marriage certificate. The Establishment decided on simply Princess Anne. But Lord Mountbatten fought every inch of the way to get Mountbatten-Windsor on the certificate. He finally persuaded the Prince of Wales to say that if Mountbatten-Windsor was not used, he, Prince Charles, would not sign the certificate. Mountbatten won his battle—a generation early.

So many questions were asked as to why this name had been used, that eventually a statement was issued saying that it had been done by the Queen's wish. Lord Beaverbrook's long held fear that Uncle Dickie's secret ambition was to make the name of British ruling house Mountbatten, was perhaps proved not to be without foundation.

Mountbatten certainly said before his dreadful death at the hands of an IRA assassin: 'My greatest happiness is that in the future royal children will be styled by the surname Mountbatten-

Windsor.' There are those who are very much convinced that it was a matter of extreme indifference to Prince Philip himself. He knew who he was.

However, while all these deliberations that led to Philip taking Lord Mountbatten's surname were going on, the Princess was not in Britain.. When, at last, the naturalization was sanctioned, she was touring South Africa with her parents, and she celebrated her 21st birthday there. She also made her first ever speech to the people of Britain and the Commonwealth, declaring that her whole life, whether it be long or short 'would be devoted to you and the service of this great Imperial Commonwealth to which we belong.'

There was one poignant moment on the tour. The royal family had climbed the high hill to the burial place of Cecil Rhodes.

'At the top,' says Brigadier Stanley Clark in his authorized version of the events of the day, 'the King stood beside the granite slab which marks the grave of Cecil Rhodes. Princess Elizabeth wandered off on her own and stood silently looking out across the desolate bush country of "World's View", the name Rhodes gave to the site. Her father watched her and said to those around him, "Poor Elizabeth. Already she is realizing that she will be alone and lonely all her life; that, no matter who she has by her side, only she can make the final decision."'

Elizabeth did her duty then, as she has always done. Even on their return home to Britain in May 1947, Prince Philip was not permitted to meet her, but nevertheless at the sight of home, she did a little jig of sheer happiness on the deck of the *Vanguard* and was, Crawfie says, radiant. The King was still in no hurry to announce the betrothal. He could not come to terms with the thought of the engagement. He felt his daughter was being hasty. His anxiety was that they, the little family of four—the royal firm of four, as he called it—would be split assunder, and so he kept reminding her that Philip was still the first young man she had ever met.

But he could not refuse her for ever. There had been a constant flow of mail to and from South Africa between Elizabeth and Philip. Their cover was blown when an official in the Palace Post Office told the press of it. The public speculation was too great for any more pretence, and besides, Philip was squiring the Princess to West End restaurants and nightclubs. They were publicly behaving like a courting couple.

At this time, Edwina Mountbatten was easing the financial strain for Philip. The Prince could not afford the sort of life that he was leading. Nightclubs were no cheaper then than they are now. He had no money of his own, and his father had left nothing, except a few debts, some clothing and a ivory-handled shaving brush which Philip had rebristled and used. There was a rumour of estates in Greece but whether or not Philip was ever granted them is uncertain.

Newspapers all over the world were acting as unwitting allies to the lovers by continuing to print that an engagement was imminent. And Elizabeth, who could be stubborn too, won her battle. In July 1947 the royal engagement was announced in the *Court Circular*. It read:

It is with the greatest pleasure that the King and Queen announce the betrothal of their dearly beloved daughter the Princess Elizabeth to Prince Philip RN, son of the late Prince Andrew of Greece and Princess Andrew (Princess Alice of Battenberg), to which union the King has gladly given his consent.

It was not gladly. It was somewhat reluctantly. The King's future son-in-law had £6 10s in the bank and his lieutenant's pay of about £11 a week. Once married he would also get a married man's allowance of £4 7s 6d. His wordly goods went easily into two suitcases, and to his valet's horror, he didn't even have a pair of decent hair-brushes. He owned three naval uniforms of varying ages, one lounge suit, a blazer and flannels, evening dress and a shooting suit, plus various odds and ends of open weave underpants and socks darned by Eileen Parker!

He had been trying to save for an engagement ring from his naval pay, and thereby giving his fellow officers the impression that he was tight with the cash. This was something of a Herculean task, considering that the royal family own probably the most priceless collection of jewels in the world. In the end, his mother, Princess Alice, supplied the engagement ring. It was made from her own engagement ring and also from one that had belonged to her grandmother. The three-carat solitaire with five smaller diamonds on either side was set in platinum.

Prince Philip brought the engagement ring to Buckingham Palace on 9 July 1947. After he had slipped it on her finger, they went to show the King and Queen. The ring was a little too large as the Prince had wanted it to be a surprise.

The young Princess pointed out to her parents that it would have to go back to the jewellers to be made smaller, adding anxiously: 'We don't have to wait until it's right, do we?'

The King laughed and shook his head.

Philip was spared the expense of a wedding ring. The people of Wales supplied a nugget of Welsh gold from which the Queen's wedding ring was made. There was sufficient left to make another for her daughter. The Queen is said never to have taken this off— though she does whizz it around on her finger when she is angry. Inside the ring is an inscription. No one knows what it says, other than the Queen, her husband and obviously the engraver. It is a secret they share.

But before the ring could be slipped on the future Queen's finger at Westminster Abbey, there was yet another detail that had to be dealt with.

Dr Geoffrey Fisher, the Archbishop of Canterbury, wrote to the King:

> Sir,
> There is a matter upon which I think I should consult your Majesty. There was a paragraph in *The Times* which said that while Lieutenant Mountbatten was baptised into the Greek Orthodox Church he appears 'always to have regarded himself as an Anglican' . . .
> In the Church of England we are always ready to minister to members of the Orthodox Church . . . No difficulty therefore arises of any sort on our side from the fact that Lieutenant Mountbatten was baptised into the Orthodox Church. At the same time unless he is officially received into the Church of England he remains formally a member of the Greek Ortho-dox Church . . . I suggest for Your Majesty's consideration that there would be an advantage if he were officially received

into the Church of England. It can be done privately and very simply . . .

Of course, the Archbishop was right. If one day Princess Elizabeth was to become the head of the Church of England, she could hardly have a Greek Orthodox husband. It took a fortnight before the Archbishop received a reply. The King had arranged with Lieutenant Mountbatten to have his position regularized. Sometime in the late summer, Prince Philip accompanied by Princess Elizabeth went quietly to Lambeth Palace. The Palace had been severely damaged in the blitz; the chapel had been gutted by fire bombs which also burned most of the library roof. A bomb had destroyed the drawing room and all the rooms above it. Most of the ceiling were down and there were few intact windows.

The original parlour of the Palace had been turned into a chapel, and it was there that Prince Philip was, in a simple five-minute ceremony, received from the Greek Orthodox Church into a full member of the Church of England.

Geoffrey Fisher asked the Prince: 'Do you believe the Church of England to be a true part of the one holy, catholic and apostolic church?'

The Prince replied: 'Yes'. He had expected to take oaths of renouncement, but having said yes, all that was left to be done was for him to take Holy Communion. Then the Archbishop entered Prince Philip's name, address, age and the date into the confirmation register.

It was only two weeks before the wedding, and naturally Geoffrey Fisher was deeply involved with that event. At tea that afternoon, Philip said jokingly to Elizabeth: 'Why not be married now? Here we both are; and there's the Archbishop!'

The event was not publicized. It was early October before the Palace Press Secretary even mentioned it, and then rather as an intimation rather than a straightforward announcement.

And *The Times*, which had started the whole thing, wrote: 'It is understood that Lieutenant Philip Mountbatten has been formally received into membership of the Church of England.'

Jumping ahead, perhaps it was as well that Philip had to take no oaths. He has little time for formal religion and was not even certain that Prince Charles should have been confirmed when he became sixteen. Throughout the ceremony at Windsor, he ostentatiously read a Bible, taking no notice of the proceedings. Archbishop Ramsey, the most gentle of men, was angry enough to say afterwards: 'Bloody rude, I call it!' Which, of course, it was.

Apart from dealing with religious matters, the Prince was also bashing up his sports car. On his mad dash from HMS *Royal Arthur* at Corsham to London, he skidded into a tree and damaged a fence, the car and himself. It was only a few bruises and a twisted knee, but the press asked sternly what would have happened if the heir to the throne had been in the car? They counselled that the Prince should never be permitted to drive the Princess. It was his first taste of the public eye fixed on his private actions. And later, when he managed to side-sweep a taxi, this time with the Princess aboard, the clamour increased.

For a man used to getting his own way, disliking criticism, and, not to put too fine a point on it, inclined to belligerence, these reports of his driving—though the Princess was convinced that on the second occasion it was all the taxi driver's fault—began his life-long battle with the Press.

And yet for his first royal engagements, accompanying the Princess to receive the Freedom of the City of Edinburgh, riding in the carriage parade at Ascot, and even making a balcony appearance, he quite enjoyed the press attention. It was not to last. He was also having to learn to walk two paces behind his fiancée, difficult for a man so competitive and determined always to lead. But he managed it splendidly just two days after the engagement at a Buckingham Palace garden party. Even his relatives said that this was throwing him to the lions, but wearing his shabby naval uniform, and accompanied by Michael Parker, he acquitted himself so well before the public that the King was delighted.

There were other, more pleasant things to learn, like eightsome reels and wearing a kilt. The reels he learned in an afternoon with help from the Princess and the King's piper, the kilt took more getting used to. The King insisted that he wore one since he was to become part of the family. Philip possessed no such thing, and was loaned one that had been owned by George V. It was too short, and feeling ridiculous, Philip dropped the King a mock curtsey. The King was not amused and told him so.

They also needed a home. The King offered them a huge beautiful house, Sunninghill Park, close to Windsor Castle. It required an enormous amount of renovation as it had been used by the army during the war.

There was muttering that it was wrong they should have a large house when so many people were homeless after the war. Perhaps it was as well that before work could begin on it, it was burned down in the summer of 1947 while the Court was at Balmoral. Instead, the King gave them Clarence House, the tumbledown Regency mansion on the Mall. But, that, too required a great deal of work—£50,000's worth—before it was properly habitable. Since both labour and materials were in short supply, like many of his new subjects, Prince Philip was going to have to start his life living with his in-laws at Buckingham Palace. And surprisingly there was the chance of them getting under each other's feet. Buckingham Palace has few private rooms. It is mostly offices and state banquetting rooms. Prince Philip, who loathes living there, calls it 'living above the shop'.

Throughout the engagement, though he was still officially living at Kensington Palace with the Dowager Duchess of Milford Haven, he was given a bachelor suite on the first floor of the Palace. It consisted of a large bedroom, a sitting room filled with Regency furniture and an oversized, old-fashioned bathroom. The Princess's suite of rooms was on the second floor.

From there he and Lilibet planned their wedding list. Baillie-Grohman was delighted to find that he and his wife were invited, and for him to be present must have been like seeing the happy ending to a pretty preposterous plot. Michael Parker and his wife were also invited. Eileen Parker had heard the announcement of the engagement on the radio. Her husband, out of the navy, was working for her grandfather's rope business in London. She rang him from their home in Scotland and told him the news. She suggested that they sent a telegram. It simply said: 'Many congratulations on your engagement. Best wishes for the future. Mike and Eileen Parker.'

To their surprise Prince Philip replied, thanking them for the telegram and saying that an invitation to the wedding would follow.

'Whilst writing,' he added, 'I would like to mention that I am considering getting some staff together and would like you to join this as a general nanny and factotum. Yours, Philip.'

It was to prove to be a momentus offer with far reaching consequences, but at that moment Mike Parker was not unnaturally delighted. So was his wife. The new job would mean that they could be together again with their small child.

The Prince and Princess worked hours deciding on a wedding guest list of 2,000 people. They were mostly personal friends or those who had performed some service for them. Eighty-year-old Miss M.J. Crewe, who had been Prince Philip's nurse, was invited, so was Helene Cordet's mother, and the American Mrs Corbina Wright, an old friend of the Prince who had sent him food parcels throughout the war.

The glaring, but hushed-up omissions were Prince Philip's sisters. All four had married Germans. One was dead, killed in a plane crash with all her family just before the war. Two had married dedicated Nazis, one of whom had bombed London, and had died in action over Italy. With the war so fresh in British memories, it seemed wiser to leave them at home. But the Prince was to sign the register with the gold pen that his sisters presented to him as a wedding present.

Nor would Philip's father be there. He had died in Monte Carlo, quietly and without fuss, of a heart attack in 1944. Before the wedding, Philip had gone to sort out his estate. There was little to do: debts to be settled and a pathetically few personal possession to be taken away. Philip's mother came to London for the wedding, and she and he together went through the suitcases. There were some good, but moth-eaten suits. Philip had them repaired and continued to wear them for some years. He was, and still is, a hoarder, carting about ancient trunks crammed with junk from his schooldays. He even kept baby clothes AND dug them out when Prince Charles was born. Once his valet, John Dean, in an unwise moment suggested that he get rid of it all.

'Certainly not,' Philip said, 'they are valuable and may be useful one day.'

But all the other relatives were there three day before the wedding, their tickets from all over Europe paid for, and their accommodation at Claridge's provided. The Palace applied for extra rations to feed 28 foreign royal guests.

On 19 November 1947, the eve of the wedding, George VI granted Prince Philip a rank and status suitable for the husband of the future Queen. At a private investiture at Buckingham Palace, King George installed him Knight Commander of the Most Noble Order of the Garter. He wore the robes that had once belonged to the late Duke of Connaught. The King, still not entirely happy about this wedding, had already invested Princess Elizabeth with the same order eight days before. He wanted her to have precedence even in this. The new Sir Philip Mountbatten was then also created Duke of Edinburgh, Earl of Merioneth and Baron Greenwich.

The dukedom was a revival of the title of Queen Victoria's second son, Alfred, Duke of Edinburgh who had helped Philip's grandfather, Prince Louis of Battenburg into the British navy. And in a curious twist, it had been this same Duke of Edinburgh who had been offered the throne of Greece when King Otto abdicated in 1862. Queen Victoria, however, would have none of it. If the Greek throne fell again, as it was certain to, her son would not be the one to tumble from it. How right she was! Events proved worse than a tumble into exile. The unfortunate Prince William of Denmark who took on the job and was crowned George I of the Hellenes, was assassinated (shot in the back) in November 1912.

After the investiture of this new Duke of Edinburgh, the King said: 'It is a great deal to give a man all at once, but I know Philip understands his responsibilities on his marriage to Lilibet.'

But what had the King really given him? A handful of titles, and not one of them 'Prince'. It seems that the Labour Prime Minister of the day, Clement Atlee, had been against that. Philip had to wait until 1957 before the Queen herself righted the omission. But the titles did ensure that the future Queen would not leave the Abbey as Princess Mrs Mountbatten.

The wedding presents started to roll in, and not all of them for the home. Philip was given not one, but two, sailing boats— *Coweslip* and *Bluebottle*. His future father-in-law gave him a brace of Purdey guns. He was given a splendid set of fishing tackle with which he once caught fifteen salmon in a day's fishing. The Aga Khan gave Lilibet a filly which she named Astrakhan, and the people of Kenya gave her a hunting lodge. Thousands of people sent clothing coupons, for clothes were still rationed in Britain. These all had to be returned. Many Americans sent nylon stockings. An American woman even sent a turkey. The refrigerator to put it in came from the WVS!

What Philip really needed was some money. Something had to be done about this new Duke of Edinburgh's finances. The man who was about to walk up the aisle to be married by the Archbishop of Canterbury was still on naval pay and had nothing else. But not until after the honeymoon was the King able to ask Parliament to make adequate provision for the heir and her husband. A select committee of Parliament, by thirteen votes to five, agreed to allocate an annuity of £10,000 to Philip, at the same time increasing the Princess's allowance to £50,000, both sums subject to income tax. The squabble over the royal finances went on for four hours, and if the Labour MPs had had their way, the sum would have been reduced to £40,000 for the two of them!

In fact the Labourites of the day were killjoys from start to finish. With postwar austerity at its worst—even bread was rationed—the Labour government felt that only an austere wedding would be acceptable to the public. They failed to see that what war-torn, grey Britain needed was a party, and an excuse for a celebration. Originally the wedding was to have taken place quietly at St George's Chapel, Windsor. Fortunately reason prevailed. Pushed by Tory and moderate Labour politicians—plus angry letters to *The Times*—the demands that the excitement and colour of a State wedding would be a welcome excuse for a bit of gaiety, caused the goverment to capitulate.

But still the wedding guest list was cut to a minimum, leaving out many politicians. Even Rab Butler didn't get an invitation.

It might well have been these omissions that caused Prince Philip to be given such a meagre allowance when the time came to fix what he was to be paid.

He was married from his grandmother's apartment at Kensington Palace and the day before his wedding he was so touchy and jittery that David Milford Haven, the best man, had to tiptoe through the rituals of this last day of bachelorhood. But jittery or not, the traditional stag party was a great success.

It was held for the bridegroom and eleven of his friends in the stylish Park Suite at the Dorchester Hotel—the same room where the Princess Elizabeth and Philip had spent the evening at a coming-out dinner the night their engagement was announced. His host was Commander George Norfolk who had been his captain on *Whelp*. The guests were young naval officers, including the best man, David Milford Haven and Lt Michael Parker who was to become his equerry. Lord Louis Mountbatten, back from what the *Daily Express* called 'giving away India', was there, too.

Marjorie Lee, the former public relations officer at the Dorchester helped organize the party. She knew most of the principals because Lord Mountbatten, the best man, Lord Milford Haven and oddly, Prince Philip's mother, were all regulars at the hotel.

'There were only twelve at the party,' she says, 'all in naval uniform and it was during the evening that the press discovered they were in the hotel. They asked if they could get pictures, so when the sweet had been served I popped upstairs and asked the head waiter if I could have a word with Lord Mountbatten as he was in charge.

'When I asked, he said: "Why not. It is a special occasion."

'The photographers came upstairs and took their pictures, and then the Duke had a bright idea. "Why don't we take a picture of them?" he said, and he got hold of the *Daily Mirror* camera and took some pictures with it, while Mike Parker took another camera and did the same.'

What Marjorie did not see was the sneaky trick that Philip and Mike Parker then played. With the cameras in their possession, they pulled out the flashbulbs and smashed them on the floor.

'Now, it's our turn to have the last laugh,' said the Prince as the photographers were ushered out.

Battle was declared and the war has continued ever since.

Marjorie Lee remembers how, once the Press had gone, the Prince decided he wanted to go down and see the chef and thank him.

'They got hold of a luggage trolley and wheeled him downstairs in the service lift from the suite to the kitchens. The chef, Jean Baptiste Virlogeux, was very surprised when the Duke arrived on a trolley, and delighted that the Duke spoke to him in French. He told him how much he had appreciated and enjoyed the meal.

'At midnight when they left, they decided that they had had such a good time they were going to try to make it an annual event, and they did have one the next year. But then Milford Haven went off to the States and the year after the Prince and Princess had gone to Malta where he was stationed, so the annual dinner died a natural death.'

That wasn't the only stag party that night. Philip moved on to a private room at the Belfry, a club off Belgrave Square with a smaller group of friends and the press were not invited. Marjorie Lee remembers the Dorchester party as being rather sedate. The Belfry affair was rather different, at least according to Milford Haven who ruined his friendship with Prince Philip by writing a newspaper article about it some years later.

'We celebrated the passing of one more good fellow into the state of matrimony with all the traditional rites and customs . . .' he said, 'while the brandy circulated and the cigar smoke grew thicker than the speech of the raconteurs . . .'

The party went on until the early hours and Milford Haven said: 'The following day I think both Prince Philip and I, staying together at Kensington Palace, felt the need of a slight stabiliser.

'Unfortunately we were due to meet a high member of the church that morning. After careful consultation we consumed only one glass of light sherry [his valet, probably more accurately, says it was a gin and tonic] apiece after breakfast.

'We felt by midmorning the effects of this tonic would have dispersed the results of the night before. But I think the venerable gentleman guessed.

'He allowed us to remain seated during most of the time we were with him, and I, for one, was profoundly grateful for his understanding.'

But nevertheless, when John Dean tapped on the Prince's door at seven o'clock on the wedding morning, the Prince woke immediately and appeared to be in great form.

He breakfasted on coffee and toast and then he dressed. John Dean in his memoirs *HRH Prince Philip: A Portrait by His Valet* tells us that he looked very fine in his uniform, on which was the insignia of a Knight Companion of the Order of the Garter. 'It was not a full-dress uniform, but the kind in which you expect to see a naval officer when you meet him in the street. The sword, which I handled so gingerly as I gave it to him, was not his own; like all the new-generation navy he did not possess one. It had belonged to his grandfather, Prince Louis of Battenberg.'

It says much for Philip's iron will that having been a heavy smoker for years, he smoked his last cigarette on the way back to Kensington Palace. He has never touched one since.

This caused something of a problem as the hung-over Milford Haven had run out and was dying for a smoke. Since Philip could not oblige, he was forced to hide his best man's outfit under an old raincoat and cycle to Kensington High Street to buy a packet.

It was a chilly morning, but a crowd had gathered outside the Palace to see the Prince leave.

'Among them was Miss Pye,' says John Dean, 'who had been with the Dowager Marchioness of Milford Haven, the Duke's grandmother, for fifty years and was her personal maid. She had known the Duke since he was a baby and he called her "Piecrust". The duke shook hands with Piecrust, with the palace sweep and other old retainers. Grinning, he ordered coffee for the shivering newspaper reporters assigned to see him start.'

He was due at the Abbey at 11.15 am, and the policeman on duty outside looked at his watch and shook his head. It was five minutes too early to leave.

When they finally did leave, they realized that they were wearing identical naval caps. David had the bigger head, and if Philip picked up the wrong one it would promptly fall over his ears. They made an ink mark inside David's so they could tell one from the other.

The service was broadcast, though there had been another argument over this. Some of the King's advisers had been worried that the service would be listened to by people drinking in public houses! And for the first time the BBC was allowed to put cameras outside the Abbey.

It was a simple service, a service which, as Dr Fisher pointed out, would have been carried out in any village church. And the Princess chose to 'obey him, serve him, love, honour and keep him in sickness and in health', insisting on the old traditional form. She believed then, as she believes now, that the principle of the husband being the head of the family is the only guarantee of happiness in the home.

She was a most beautiful bride in an incandescent gown of pearl-coloured slipper satin embroidered in crystals and pearls. Her train had three layers of tulle and was fifteen feet long. Her new husband could not have failed to be moved by how enchanting and how happy she looked as she walked up the aisle to stand beside him.

Colour came back to London with the processions. Crowds in front of the Palace cheered and called for the young couple to come to the balcony. Masses lined the route to watch them drive in the ceremonial landau to Waterloo Station for their departure on honeymoon. It was in Whitehall, when Philip, cheerfully waving back, received a nudge in the ribs from his bride. Just in time, his hand came up to deliver a perfect salute to the Cenotaph.

It was a glittering day, particularly for Lord Louis Mountbatten. He and his elegant wife had caught every eye in the Abbey. He was a proud man when he heard the future Queen take his family's name.

'This was,' he wrote later, 'a great moment in the history of our family.'

Surprisingly for such a vain man, he forebore to add that the moment had been created by his own efforts.

6

THE WOMEN IN HIS LIFE

In those years of long-distance courtship as she began to grow up, it is inconceivable that Princess Elizabeth did not realize that the Prince with his good looks and strong personality would not encounter other women. And, of course, he did. Though he seems to have been careful never to become deeply involved. Most of his feminine companionship was found either away from Britain or under the sheltering umbrella of his relatives' homes.

Two of the women with whom he spent much time (both of whom wrote books to prove it), throw up their hands in horror at the thought that there should have been anything more than a jolly, happy platonic friendship with the young Greek Prince. Indeed, at times one feels that both Queen Alexandra of Yugoslavia and the cabaret artiste, Helene Cordet, protest too much.

If, reading between the lines in Queen Alexandra's account of her grown-up encounters with Philip, her readers came to the conclusion that she was for a while close to the Prince, or at least wanted to be, she has only herself to blame. Most certainly her more-than-cousinly interest in him shines through, while she unwittingly reveals a strong resentment of Uncle Dickie.

Did Uncle Dickie's machinations spoil her chances with the Viking Prince? Though undoubtedly she was more than consoled by her marriage to King Peter of Yugoslavia (then the Crown Prince, and on royal balance a much better catch) a note of regret, even a touch of jealousy, scents the book of this royal born, lively woman.

By 1939 the little girl whose family had welcomed the homeless

Prince Philip had grown into an exciting young woman, slim, with long dark hair, and the long thin face and dark eyes of a Modigliani portrait.

Their first grown-up encounter was when Alexandra's mother, Queen Aspasia, invited Philip to spend his summer holidays with them in Venice when he was 17 years old.

Philip's father found the prospect alarming and reminded his sister-in-law that Philip still had to pass his exams, and to keep him out of girl trouble.

Alexandra says that at this time she detected undertones of complete heartlessness in her cousin, perhaps because he was squiring blondes, brunettes and redheaded charmers quite impartially—but not Alexandra.

The summer was a round of parties, and at 11 Queen Aspasia would indicate her desire to go home. 'But,' says Alexandra, 'there was always some lovely young thing in tulle or organdie to whom Philip suggested they should give a lift home. "There's no need to keep the driver, Auntie Aspasia," he would say. "I'll take over. The boatman's had a long day".'

He got away with it on the stipulation that he was back in twenty minutes.

Then one particular girl took his eye, and he begged his Aunt to let them stay out longer.'Mummy,' says Alexandra, 'was fully aware of the heady perils of Venice . . . "Very Well," she agreed, "but you are to cruise round and round and the island and don't stop the engine. I shall be listening".'

After three or four circles, the phut-phut-phut of the engine stopped. There was five minutes of silence.

'We had trouble with the sparking plugs,' Philip explained the next day.

The war did a great deal for Princess Alexandra's friendship with the young Prince. On 10 June 1940, Prince Philip's nineteenth birthday, Italy invaded Greece. Alexandra, who had been staying in Italy, fled home to Athens. In Italy she had suddenly become an enemy alien. It was hardly the time for the royal family to be away when their country was at war.

'Suddenly, Philip turned up in Athens,' trills Alexandra, 'gay, debonair, confident . . .'

79

Greece was not yet occupied and Alexandra's mother had found a house on an Athenian hilltop. There was no place to park a car . . . 'but Philip would come bounding up the hundred steps, ready for gramophone records and fun, and dancing with a whole new group of friends . . .' Alexandra wrote.

'. . . In the evenings the family often gathered either at the Palace with the King (Uncle Georgie) or at one of our homes. We never knew when Philip would join us. When the air-raids began we were supposed to go to a shelter . . . but instead we went to the roof-garden and watched . . . Philip contributed a running commentary amid the bark of the ack-ack guns, the flutter of searchlights and the roar of the bombers.'

As the war hotted up in the Balkans, the Greek royal family moved itself first to Crete and then to Alexandria in Egypt.

Alexandra writes: 'One morning when mummy and I were at breakfast we heard a familiar whistle and outside our window Philip and David [Milford Haven, the Prince's cousin and boy-hood friend] assailed us with whoops of glee.

'I had to admit I had been worrying about Philip. Now we were all three together again, ready to do the town. We went out to a swimming pool or beach and splashed happily in the sun.

'Philip had contrived to get hold of an absurdly small car which streaked through the streets with the noise of a thousand demons. For the first time I found my two cousins handsome and attractive beaux. I liked David's lazy smile and I liked Philip's broad grin.

'At all events I was distressed at leaving them behind when we were ordered to move to the comparative safety of Cairo.

'But Philip soon tracked us to Shepheard's Hotel. In his little wasp of a car we went out to the Ghezira Club, swam or just talked through the long lazy afternoons when he was off duty. We explored the old bazaars and the magnificent botanical gardens, or in a chatty mood went to Groppi's for tea. Philip used to talk even at this time of a home of his own, a country house in England he had planned to the last detail of fitments and furniture. This is so like Philip; once he has made up his mind on anything he knows precisely where he is going, determined to make every plan come true.'

Queen Alexandra may not have been part of that long-term

plan, but when she sailed for South Africa and safety with King George II of the Hellenes, Philip was there at Port Said to see them off. And after only a week or two staying at General Smuts' home near Cape Town, there was Philip again, having been transfered to a troopship which seems to have almost followed the route of the liner that was conveying the Greek royals.

One evening in Cape Town Alexandra wanted to chat, but Philip insisted on finishing a letter he was writing. She asked who he was writing to.

'Lilibet,' he replied.

'Who?' she asked, rather mystified.

'Princess Elizabeth in England.'

'But she's only a baby!' said Alexandra, and then decided that since Philip was going to England he was angling for invitations, a not unreasonable assumption since Philip was usually angling for invitations.

Perhaps it was a comforting thought.

By the time Philip was back in England towards the end of 1941, so were Alexandra and her mother. They stayed at the Ritz Hotel, before finding an apartment of their own in Grosvenor Square.

A frequent visitor was Philip, who came to lunch, took his cousin to the 400 Club or the Savoy, or visiting their cousin Marina at the Duchess of Kent's country home in Buckinghamshire.

'I best remember,' says Alexandra, 'Philip on furlough, Philip dining and dancing and confiding . . .'

The other woman in his life at this time was the second childhood friend, Helene Foufounis, who was to become better known as Helene Cordet. She had grown to be a small, vivacious woman with the face of a friendly pekinese and a megawatt personality.

Her relationship with Philip, it could be said, helped her considerably in forging her career as a cabaret artiste, a television star and then a nightclub queen in England. Though she would protest when his name was used in her publicity, it was certainly no bad thing in making her famous.

The story that the British press latched upon was that Prince

Philip is godfather to her children, Max and Louise. Her grandchildren, one of whom is called Philip, attend Prince Philip's old school Gordonstoun, as did their father before them, and not without a little help from the Prince.

If that sounds like innuendo, Madame Cordet says she has lived with it all her life. In the late fifties and early sixties, the London cognoscenti, as uninformed as they believe themselves to be informed, swore that Helene's two children, Max and Louise, had been fathered by Prince Philip. That, she says, is not true, but the story may have gained credence because they were born out of wedlock. Out of necessity at that less tolerant time, she was forced to make a mystery of their parentage. She had been deeply in love with the father, Max Boisot, a French airforce officer in wartime England but he deserted her and the children, though she says they are now reconciled.

'At the time I asked Prince Philip if I should sue those people [who were suggesting that the Prince was her lover]' she says. 'It used to make me really mad, not so much for me, as for the Royal family. It wasn't right, that chit-chat. So I said to Philip, "what do I do?" He said: "Look, if you like you can sue them but I don't think it's worth it. On the contrary, it will just stir up more trouble".'

Helene says that her mother always knew that Princess Elizabeth could become Philip's wife.

'I don't think she ever had it in mind for me,' she said. 'She always wanted the Royal family to remain Royal. But she used to say that Philip wanted to act like a fairy Godmother to me to repay our family in some way or another.'

And over the years he has been a good and loyal friend to her and her children. They were invited to most of the children's parties given for Charles and Anne.

'I suppose I stopped seeing Philip when I was about eleven or twelve, and then I saw him again in England when I was about eighteen. He would have been about fourteen or fifteen, and when I first laid eyes on him after all those years, I thought Oh God! He had been so beautiful as a child and now he was growing up. It gave me a bit of a shock. His nose was bigger, everything was bigger.'

82

Helene had come to London with her mother after her step-father's death. It was her stepfather, a patron of the Greek royal family who picked up the tabs for Philip and his family for part of the time when they lived in France. The family fortunes that had so helped Philip's family were seriously depleted and they were living in a flat in Princes Square, Bayswater. But Helene's mother, a strong royalist, had carefully and consistently nurtured her relationship with the Prince. Thus the young Helene entered into a lifelong friendship with Philip which has never faltered.

'He would go off to Greece and bring me back huge jars of Greek jam,' Madame Cordet recalls. 'As a teenager he was very agreeable. A very nice boy. He was very self-assured. I think Gordonstoun was a very good training. I sent my own son there afterwards and saw the same thing. It's changed since. It's not as tough as it was. My mother wanted my son to go to Winchester, but Philip wrote to me and asked if I really wanted that.'

The young Max went to Gordonstoun. Philip's old school, just as Prince Charles, Prince Andrew and Prince Edward did later.

'Philip and I had kept in touch over the years.' Madame Cordet said. 'He was the best man AND gave me away at my first wedding.'

Prince Philip was only 16 at the time. Helene was 20 and her first husband, William Neal Kirby was a 23-year-old student. They met at Oxford where they were both studying. The legal marriage took place in a registry office in Oxford, but there was a second ceremony at the Greek Orthodox Church in Bayswater. Helene, stunning in bridal white came up the aisle on the arm of an earnest, thin, fair Prince Philip, who gave her away—after holding up proceedings by treading on her veil.

It is perhaps unfortunate for Helene and Prince Philip that it is not possible to completely scotch the rumours concerning her children's parentage.

It's impossible to prove that he could *not* have been the children's father; it's equally impossible to prove that he is.

The marriage to William Kirby was not a success. It was all over in two years and after that Helene's recollection of events in her book *Born Bewildered*, becomes blurred. She says they did not get on, drifted apart and decided to go their own separate ways.

In her book she does not actually name Marcel Boisot as the father of her two love children but talks of being madly in love with a French serviceman. She became pregnant in March 1943 at the time when Prince Philip was in Britain and often in London, sailing between Rosyth and Sheerness. Her son, Max, was born on 11 December 1943, at the Hayside Nursing Home in Maidenhead and registered as William Kirby's child.

Though they had been apart for two years, she had not yet divorced Kirby. When he decided to make their parting legal he cited Lieutenant Marcel Henri Boisot as the co-respondent. On 27 November 1944, the marriage was dissolved.

Helene was already pregnant again and had been since July 1944. She had conceived when her baby boy was seven months old. Prince Philip had been in London since November 1943 while his ship was refitted. He joined the new destroyer *Whelp* in May 1944, but did not sail from Plymouth for the Far East until 4 August.

On 17 January 1945 (just two months after her divorce from Kirby) Marcel and Helene married at Paddington Registry Office. Twenty-two days later, on 8 February 1945, her daughter Louise Margaret Helene was born at home in Wraysbury. Helene's mother registered the birth.

She and Boisot barely had any married life together. He was sent to Egypt with the French airforce almost immediately after the war ended in May. The intention was that she should follow him, but it never happened. He left Helene destitute in Paris while her two children lived with her mother in England. When he returned, he did so with another woman. The marriage that had hardly begun was over, like so many wartime unions.

But curiously it was not until 1962, many years after Boisot and Helene parted, that the Frenchman saw fit to declare in the Somerset House register of births in London that Max was his child.

Only then, when the boy was 18, did his name become legally Boisot. It was also the year when Helene Cordet published her first autobiography, and the year when her fame in Britain was at its height.

Today, her son Max Boisot is a 45-year-old businessman,

working in China and Prince Philip still keeps in touch with him. This is unusual since normally he keeps in touch with his many godchildren only until they are 21.

'Philip saw Max when he and the Queen went to China, because Max wrote to him and asked him to visit.' Madame Cordet said. 'One reporter wrote about the fact that Philip vanished on the trip to the Great Wall. The reason he did that was to see Max.'

But in wartime Britain, before Helene's second marriage, she and her mother continued to entertain Prince Philip when he came to London on leave.

'He came to our flat once or twice,' she recalls. 'The flat was not very nice, but mother never felt bad about the less marvellous surroundings in which we lived. At one point we had no furniture. Our mattresses were on the floor. We were really poor. I was trying to work as a bit-part actress.

'By then the King had gone back to Greece so Philip must have had some funds, being a Greek prince, and once or twice we went out. We went with him to a club in his midshipman's uniform and he signed his name as Philip of Greece, and the club manager, who was getting annoyed thinking he was being clever, had to receive an explanation from me that it was true.

'I saw him a few times during the war. Socially we got on fine. I was older, but didn't look it.

In April 1945 Madame Cordet went to Paris to join her husband who was immediately sent to Cairo.

In September Boisot wrote asking for a divorce, and then followed months of misery and sheer grinding poverty as Helene searched for a job in a Paris which was not gay at the aftermath of the war.

It was not long after this, early in 1946, when Prince Philip appeared in Paris. Helene Cordet believes that her mother had told him about her troubles and he had come to cheer her up. The first thing he did was to invite her to tea at the Ritz.

He arrived on a woman's bicycle that was much too small for him. The Greek Embassy in Paris had offered to loan him a car but he felt that this was not necessary—cars were in short supply in Paris. So he borrowed a bike from the secretary of a naval friend. After tea, he and Helene decided to race each other, he on the bike and she on the Metro from Place de la Concorde to rue Pierre Charron.

Helene won the race, and pleased with herself, watched as he pedalled like mad down Champs-Elysées towards her, his knees almost under his chin.

They also drove up Champs-Elysées together in a horse-drawn cab. Helene suggested they should walk, thinking of the Prince's naval pay. But he insisted they ride.

After a few minutes, Philip folded his arms and said: 'Hm, just look at us. A romantic thing like a fiacre and here we are just two old friends.'

'He took me to the Lancaster Hotel to eat,' she recalls, 'and my six-year-old jacket was very frayed. I went to take my jacket off, and suddenly remembered the fraying and kept it on. He asked me why I had changed my mind, and I explained.

'He said, "Nonsense! take it off," and he hung it on the back of the chair, insisting I was the best dressed woman in Paris, which was rather nice of him, because I wasn't.'

When the news of the engagement of Princess Elizabeth to Prince Philip broke, the French press was as over-excited as the British. It had scented the presence of a mystery blonde with whom the Prince had spent a great deal of time on his last visit to Paris and wrote a great many stories asking who she could be. Helene Cordet says she was amazed to realize that SHE was the mystery blonde.

Which is perhaps why only Helene's mother was invited to the royal wedding.

But, come the Coronation, Helene, her mother and her children were all invited to Buckingham Palace. They were to be there at eight to see the start and finish of the procession from the Palace and watch the ceremony on TV. They stayed until seven in the evening in company with the entire royal family. At the end of the day the Queen walked down the corridor dressed in her robes and crown to greet everyone.

Astonishingly, Helene cut this once-in-a-lifetime occasion, sending her mother and children without her. Why, one wonders?

'I missed it because I overslept,' she explained. 'I was working in the variety theatre in those days and I came home about six in the morning and went to bed. I slept to three p.m. and then the Coronation was all over. It was naughty of me because we were all looking forward to it, but I was so tired I just couldn't make it.

'My mother and the children went and Philip turned around to my mother and said: "What have you done to Helene?" When my mother said I was home asleep, he was a bit shocked.

'My daughter created a hoo-ha because in the room next to the balcony there was Georgie Porgy, one of the young foreign Princes and she was running about with him. And then she went to the window. There were seats all around the Victoria Monument, and people saw Louise at window and thought she was Princess Anne. They all cheered and she waved like mad back. She was even televised.

'I finally met the Queen officially at her Jubilee. My daughter was pregnant at the time, and I was with her, my granddaughter, my son-in-law and my son. The Queen came up and said, "Are these all yours? I've heard so much about you." She was very sweet, and then Philip came up and said: "The girls all look blooming".'

Madame Cordet may only have met the Queen once, but over the years she has visited the Palace and the Prince many times. She went to Prince Philip's fiftieth birthday party and Prince Charles and Princess Anne invited her and her children to the Jubilee party that they threw for their parents.

'One day we were at Buck House,' she said, 'and the doorman took us up in the lift to Philip's private rooms. He went one floor further up than he should have to the Queen's apartments and began apologising profusely. Philip said this is obviously one trying to get above one's station.

'I introduced my two granddaughters to Philip last July and the older one, aged seventeen, was very provocative. She was wearing all her badges, anti-apartheid, etc. She came out with arguments about South Africa. She was into all sorts of causes and things and reading the *Guardian*. She made Philip laugh. He told her to keep an open mind.

'We stayed about an hour at the Palace in his private rooms.

He was very relaxed. Abigail, the youngest, didn't say much. I also had my daughter, Louise's little one. She said she was bored, so I shh'd her. But she was only nine years old.'

Another artiste whose name was linked with Prince Philip in those early days was the glamorous Pat Kirkwood. Dark haired, with beautiful legs, she was known as the Champagne girl of the forties and fifties. She starred in a stream of hit musicals, was given a Hollywood film contract, and eventually her own TV show.

And the Cognoscenti said that she was Prince Philip's mistress. Again they were wrong. Now 65-years old, still stunning looking, she lives in quiet retirement, happily married to her fourth husband. And her one and only night out with Prince Philip is indelibly etched on her memory.

'It was in 1948, and at the time I was having quite a lively social life,' she said. 'As much as I could because I was appearing twice nightly at the London Palladium in Starlight Roof with Val Parnell.

'I met everyone because I was sort of unofficially engaged to Baron, the Royal photographer. He was an absolute darling, and a great friend of Prince Philip's.

'Baron and I had a date for after the show at eleven o'clock. He had said: "Let's go out on the town and you get dressed up and we'll have a really nice evening."

'I had a gorgeous dress I had brought back from New York with me. It was sort of corally orange in fine wool. It was long, draped to one side with a black velvet rose. It was gorgeous and I looked good in it.

'I waited and waited for Baron. Eleven o'clock came, quarter past, half past. I was furious, pacing around, and then the phone rang in my dressing room. It was Baron. He said: "Sorry about being late, I don't want to say any more, but there are to be three of us."

'I clicked. I thought, oh my goodness, he's bringing Prince Philip. The way he said it—I knew.

'I wasn't in a state. I was cross about being kept waiting when I was hungry. I'd done two shows and I wanted my supper. I'd been looking forward to a night on the town with my boyfriend, so I wasn't particularly thrilled at all really.

'They arrived at the stage door, Prince Philip, Baron and the Prince's equerry, a young man in Naval uniform they called Basher. The fireman was on duty because the stage door man had gone home. "You can't come in at this time of night," he said. And then he saw Prince Philip and the poor fellow nearly fainted.

'My dresser, who was still waiting with me was an enormous fat, marvellous woman called Bessie Porter. She was very cockney and adored the Royal family. I hadn't told her anything, thinking it would be a nice surprise.

'Well, when Prince Philip walked into my dressing room, she went scarlet from her neck right up to her forehead—and did this damn curtsey in the middle of the floor.

'Philip could hardly get in the door because she nearly filled the entire floor. But she was thrilled.

'Anyway, I was introduced to Philip and then off we went. Prince Philip insisted that I went in his car. They'd all had a marvellous lunch, but they weren't tanked up because by this time it was half-past-eleven at night. I said I wanted to drive, but he wouldn't have it. And we drove off down Piccadilly for Les Ambassadeurs and there was a car in front, he kept hooting his horn and saying: "Come on! Let's get on now!"

'When we got to Les Ambassadeurs it was very late. The Maitre d' then was a Mr Williams and when Baron said we wanted to a table for four, Williams turned around and said: "Now look here, Mr Baron, I've told you before about coming here at this time. We are absolutely packed out and there is no room. We've just played The King."

"Then tell them to play it again," said Philip. Mr Williams turned to tell this impertinent fellow off, saw who it was and feebly said: "Yes, just come this way, please."

'So we floated in. It was terribly funny because everyone was there that night. I remember Jean Simmons, Margaret Lockwood, Michael Wilding—all theatre was there. It was packed. And there I floated in in my orange dress with Prince Philip and Baron.

'They'd had their meal, and they said: "I suppose you don't want anything to eat." I said: "I certainly do. I'm hungry. I want my dinner."

'So I sat there and I ate, and everything stopped. There was dead silence and everyone stared.

'Philip wanted to go on somewhere, so we went upstairs to the Milroy nightclub. Philip said: "What are we going to have? Let's have some beer." I said: "Beer! I don't want beer! I want champagne!" I thought here I am with Prince Philip and Baron and I'm certainly not drinking beer. So I had some champagne, and then Philip asked me to dance.

'And we danced . . . and we danced . . . and we danced . . . and we had such laughs. He was so amusing. But the funny thing was that the orchestra had just finished backing me at the Hippodrome. It was a Latin American band and Santos, the bandleader was standing there with the maracas, and there I came dancing by with Prince Philip. "Hubba! Hubba!" he said, which was a 1949 equivalent of Wow!

'We stayed on the dance floor for about an hour. He wouldn't let me sit down. We danced anything they played, foxtrots, sambas—it was ballroom dancing in those days. We got on like a house on fire. He told me not to bother saying Sir or Prince Philip or your highness or anything.

'The dance floor was packed. The awful thing was people kept piling in. They were coming to look at Prince Philip dancing with Pat Kirkwood. Everyone was looking at us, and I said: "Don't you think we ought to sit down?"

'He didn't want to. Then he started impersonating the expressions of the people coming in. What I didn't know was that they were from the Court.

'But he still went on dancing, and old Baron got the hump. He disappeared for about half-an-hour. He was sulking. But when he came back we sat down and then I danced with Baron, and we stayed there until they put the chairs on the tables.

'Then we went back to Baron's place and Baron cooked scrambled eggs. During the meal in walked a little fellow who was called Otto. He was Baron's apprentice and he was staying there. He had his very young, pretty girl-friend with him. She was introduced to us all, and she just gasped. She was stunned. She looked as if something had hit her very hard.

90

'She sat down and stared at Prince Philip and she never said a word for the rest of the evening.

'We all had a marvellous time. We wound up in the early hours and then Philip went off with Basher. Baron drove me home to St John's Wood where I had a flat with my mother. Even though I was 26, she was going hairless. It was 6.30 in the morning.

'It was a marvellous evening; really wonderful. I could certainly have had a crush on the Prince if he hadn't been married to Princess Elizabeth. He was lovely, and very good looking. But the repercussions afterwards were terrible.

'It went round that I was Prince Philip's mistress.

'My dear Bessie was in the Odeon Cinema one afternoon, and newsreels of Prince Philip came on. The woman in front said to her friend: "Of course you know he's got another woman already. It's that actress, Pat Kirkwood." And this sort of gossip went on for years and years.

'I think Baron eventually lost his commission. There was a terrible to-do. Apparently the King sent for Prince Philip and gave him a dressing down. But it had only been innocent fun. We weren't dancing cheek to cheek. He was out on a night with the boys and I just happened to be there. It didn't seem to alter his friendship with Philip. And it wasn't Baron's fault. Philip should have known better than to go dancing around the place when his wife was at Balmoral. I don't know if it upset Princess Elizabeth, I imagine it upset the King more, because there was Prince Philip in the middle of the dance floor making fun of everyone . . . mimicking all the court. And they did all look aghast and shocked.

'I saw him again when I did a TV command performance. It was the first TV command performance there had been, and we all stood in line and I was presented to him and the Queen.

'He was so naughty. He came along and said as he stood in front of me: "I did enjoy myself that evening." I said: "Oh, good." But it sounded awful. And of course it was just what everyone was waiting to hear.

'Years later, in 1952, I'd married my second husband, Spiro Gabriele [a shipping company director] and I met a chum of mine. She said: "Do you know, my husband went into White's

Club the other day and a member there said: 'I do think it's a bit much of Prince Philip. He's given Pat Kirkwood a white Rolls Royce.' "

'I just roared with laughter. I went out and told my husband and he laughed and said: "Well, if he has, darling, will you get it out and let's use it."

'I saw the Prince once more. Years later, around the end of the 1960's there was a big concert at the Theatre Royal, Drury Lane. Philip was attending. An actress in the dressing room said: "It will be an exciting night for you, meeting Prince Philip again."

I said: "I'm jolly well fed-up with all this," so I got them altogether and told them exactly what had happened, right down to the scrambled eggs. But they all said: "Come on! And the rest of it!" They didn't believe me.

'Prince Philip came along the line and stopped at me. He said: "Hello," and I said "Hello." Then he asked, "when did you play Drury Lane before?"

'I said: "I did a Jack Hylton memorial concert," and that's all I said because they were all watching. He moved on, looking a bit cross because I was so frozen. Then he came back and said: "Is it the same?"

'"Practically," I said, and that was it.'

It would seem that the King's terrible dressing down worked. Because though the Prince has always liked women, and had many women friends over the years, never have any of his encounters been so public since.

But whispers of the Prince's penchant for pretty ladies have never really died away, and when Tory MP Anthony Beaumont-Dark declared in the House of Commons that Prince Philip knew more about adultery than he did, there was, as you might expect, a deafening silence from Buckingham Palace.

Prince Philip did not see fit to react to Mr Beaumont-Dark's comment even if it had been rather sneakily made in the privileged atmosphere of the House of Commons.

Later, a defiant Mr Beaumont-Dark said he had nothing to repent. 'It was,' he pointed out, 'Prince Philip who had used the word adultery, not me.'

It was all a bit of a fuss over nothing. Prince Philip, defending his position as one who spends his weekend blasting birds out of the sky at the same time as lecturing us on the preservation of wild life had said to a critic of this double-think: 'Are you saying that adultery is all right, provided you don't enjoy it?' Mr Beaumont-Dark, as politicians do, had decided to make capital out of this.

But adultery and Prince Philip? Could this be? There is no evidence at all, but there is plenty of evidence that the Queen's husband likes attractive women. He harmlessly flirts with women, mostly those from his own circle. He likes to dance and he feels safe dancing with the wives of his closest friends.

Even today, there is still chat about how very taken the Prince once was with Susie Ferguson, who is now Mrs Hector Barrantes. There is, perhaps, some irony here in that Susie's daughter is our Fergie, Duchess of York, and Susie's ex-husband, Major Ronald Ferguson, is Prince Charles's polo manager.

Their marriage was, in any case, shaky. The stunningly elegant and sexy Susie with a toss of her long mane of hair, ran off with Señor Hector Barrantes, a professional polo player from Argentina. She settled in the Argentine in 1975, leaving her daughters Sarah and Jane with their father. Curiously, she was following in the footsteps of Princess Diana's mother who also ran away with someone she found more exciting.

Prince Philip's polo-playing days, and the parties that went on after the match made a perfect opportunity for the little 'flirts' that probably livened up a privileged, but routine and rather stereotyped life. But he would never do anything to compromise the Queen. It has been his life's work to protect her as far as he possibly can.

In 1962 the Prince went to Buenos Aires to play polo on an unofficial visit. He was staying with the British Ambassador, but after an early bed, he would leave the embassy and go partying with the polo crowd until the early morning.

'Of course he likes women,' his old friend Helene Cordet says angrily. 'He is like his father was. I know he has that reputation. But if a man doesn't look at a women, what happens? Let us not forget that some people say other things, completely the contrary, and that it is terrible. What the hell can he do to have a decent reputation? If he doesn't look at women, they say he likes men. He likes women. So what. It's a good thing.'

'He likes the company of women,' one royal watcher said. You can see it at cocktail parties. He makes a bee line for some good-looking girl and won't be interested in talking to anyone else.

'There was a cocktail party for the press in the middle of the royal tour of Jordan in 1985 in Amman. One of the guests was a very attractive American girl, tall, slim and rangy, who did not realize that the correct wear for the occasion was a cock-tail dress.

'She came to the reception in tight jeans, long boots and a T-shirt, and looking very sexy indeed.

'We all thought that the Queen and Philip would ignore her, but he spotted her immediately. He got her in a corner and kept going back to talk to her. It was obvious that he liked what he saw!

'But then he's always been like that before and after his marriage, and yet this has no effect at all on the very deep relationship that he and the Queen share. You have to remember that he has always been a show-off, even as a boy, and it's more fun to show off to an attractive woman than to a group of men. And there aren't too many women who aren't deeply flattered when his eye lights on them. He may be 66, but he is still a marvellous looking man. Always was, probably always will be.

'But at the end of the day, nothing or no one would ever come between him and the Queen. They are still in love, but more important, they are good friends. They still have a lot to say to each other.'

Insiders say that his closest confidante for the past twelve years or so has been tall, elegant Princess Alexandra. She is his second cousin, though the age gap between them is more of uncle proportions. Both come from the Greek royal family and share a common heritage and family.

In court circles it is common knowledge that they have always been close. He was very fond of Alexandra when she was a small girl. Her mother, Princess Marina, Duchess of Kent, was his close ally in helping along his marriage to the future Queen, and latterly Princess Alexandra has had some problems with her marriage. For many years now, her husband has suffered from crippling back pain and kidney troubles.

It is said that she and Prince Philip have come to rely on each other for friendship and support. And it is not really surprising that he should have chosen Princess Alexandra as a companion. She is the most popular member of the royal family, much loved by everyone. She shares Philip's interest in sailing, and plays hostess for the Prince on *Britannia* at Cowes Week each year— the Queen never goes to Cowes. They swim together in the Windsor Castle pool—a form of exercise which is helpful to Prince Philip's severe arthritis. Alexandra's businessman husband, Angus Ogilvy, is said to feel pangs of jealousy at the depth of the friendship between the two of them, but it is accepted in the royal family that Alexandra and the Prince have a special relationship.

Since the close men friends of his youth, a polyglot collection that the Queen used to refer to as 'Philip's funny friends', went out of his life, Philip seems to have turned more to women for companionship. Few of his men friends are left.

Which is perhaps as well, for his men friends caused him more trouble than any of his women friends ever has.

7

AFTER THE HONEYMOON

The honeymoon was not a great success. Broadlands, Lord Louis' country home at Romsey, was too accessible to the public and too near to London. Philip, unused to the curiosity which royalty inspires in the British must have thought that half of London had come to gawp at them. They only stayed at Broadlands for a week, but that week was like a siege, with people climbing trees, walls, anything mountable, to get a look at the honeymooners. John Dean, the Duke's valet was horrified by it all. He reported that at Romsey Abbey where the royal couple went for Sunday morning service, people seemed to go mad, climbing over tombstones to peer through the windows . . .

'A thousand people went to the Abbey that morning, and a good proportion of them were there to peer rather than to worship. Those who could not get in carried chairs, ladders, even a sideboard into the churchyard to stand on in order to get a glimpse of the honeymooners. It was rather a shocking performance.'

The Press were also there in force, and their cameras enraged Philip. He had not learned, and has never learned, that the British weren't giving him £10,000 a year for nothing. He was now public property.

Returning to London they issued to statement which bears the unmistakable stamp of the barely concealed sarcasm of Philip.

The reception given to us on our wedding day and the loving interest shown by our fellow countrymen and well-wishers have left an impression that will never grow faint. We can find no words to express what we feel, but we can at least offer our grateful thanks to the millions who have given us this unforgettable send-off in our married life.

The couple finished off their honeymoon at Balmoral. Philip had a cold.

Back at Buckingham Palace, while they waited for Clarence House to be refurbished, the Duke was given a bedroom in the Princess's apartment with a sitting room between her room and his. The man who had been homeless now by right was entitled to enjoy many. Windsor, Balmoral, Sandringham, Craigowan, Wood Farm, apart from Windlesham Moor, a comfortable, quite ordinary but five-bedroomed house with servants' quarters, off the Bagshot-Sunningdale road which was to be the Edinburgh's weekend home for the time being.

One of the first things that Philip had done when he became engaged to Princess Elizabeth was to shift around the furniture in her apartments to be more comfortable. Once married he altered things around even more, and he gained enormous pleasure from the furnishing of Windlesham.

Windlesham was the smallest house the Princess had ever lived in, but it was the first home that Philip could genuinely call his own. He spent a lot of time making it attractive with wedding presents, hanging pictures himself and moving the furniture to its best advantage. He panelled the walls of his study with maple wood that was a wedding present from Canada, and which hid store cupboards and a bookcase that opened up to reveal a filing cabinet. He wanted to pay for everything himself at Windlesham, but on £10,000 a year and his naval pay, he could not afford to hire the number of staff that his wife was used to. For a while he used to rope in his detective to help with the chores, but eventually his wife put her foot down and brought two footman from the Palace and paid their wages herself.

He went back to work at the Admiralty which was hardly arduous as he was given so much time off for other engagements. Every weekend was spent at Windlesham, where he constructed a cricket pitch where there had once been a tennis court and invited weekend guests, including Michael Parker, who were keen cricketers. Their opponents were usually local teams.

They had to wait until 4 July (Independence Day Philip called it) before they could move into their Clarence House home. They had watched its refurbishing closely, visiting it sometimes twice a day. Again there was not much to buy—the wedding presents and the 'stores' at Buckingham Palace providing most of what was needed.

Philip put a lot of energy into Clarence House in the period when he was forced to live at the Palace. He was bored at the Admiralty, referring to his job as shuffling papers. He was determined to carry on with his naval career and saw no reason why this should be impossible. The King was only 52 years of age. He thought he would be a free man for many years yet. There were official things that he had to do. He was given special leave for occasions like the highly successful State visit that he and the Princess made to Paris in 1948 while she was pregnant with Charles, but he was reluctant to relinquish what he liked doing best—being a sailor.

He took a staff course at Greenwich Royal Naval College, and opted to live in along with the other officers there. It was probably preferable to life in Buckingham Palace which depressed him. He loathed the number of the servants and the protocol and made no bones about letting them know it. He was considered arrogant and difficult by both staff and household. Apologists for him point out that he had not been brought up to a ceremonial existence, and one in which he took second place to his wife. But one might say that he was surely too intelligent not to realize that this was the price of marrying the heir presumptive. And the choice had been his.

At this same time he had begun to work seriously as an officer of the National Playing Fields Association. He began as the organization's president in 1949 and did a brilliant fund-raising job for them. He was inundated with requests to be patron of this or that, make a speech, make an appearance, and that has never changed.

He began to write his own speeches, and trenchant they were. His speeches were originally written for him by his comptroller,

Lt General Sir Frederick 'Boy' Browning. He rather publicly made his opinion of Boy Browning's speeches clear when he ostentatiously put Browning's notes to one side and produced a sheaf of his own. Boy Browning was never again invited to write a speech and it seems unlikely that he would volunteer.

However, it's hard not to have some sympathy for Prince Philip if the standard of speeches was like that of his first, when he received the freedom of the city of London. He said:

'The ideal that my wife and I have set before us is to make the utmost of the special opportunities we have, to try to bring home to our generation the full importance of that contribution.'

Maybe it sounded better when he said it.

He was a happy man in these years, even though the ill-health of the King put an extra burden of work on him and Elizabeth. And the happiest year was 1948 when his first-born son arrived on 14 November. Prince Philip had been a bundle of nerves all day and all his public duties had been cancelled.

Two Harley Street consultants attended the birth in the Buhl Room of the Palace. The King and Queen waited anxiously in the ante-room.

Philip waited with them for a while, but became increasingly restless. Mike Parker suggested a game of squash. Philip changed into a pair of flannels and a roll-neck sweater and they went to the squash court in the Palace and then for a swim in the pool. They were just drying themselves when Sir Alan Lascelles, the King's private secretary, came with the news that the Princess had given birth to a healthy 7lb 6oz baby boy. It was his father who chose the name Charles as a breakaway from the more obvious family names.

With wet hair, both rushed to the room where the grandparents were already receiving compliments. Michael Parker had champagne ready. The Prince had been delivered by forceps, and by the time the Princess had come around from the anaesthetic Parker also produced an enormous bouquet of roses and carnations ready for Prince Philip to present.

Five thousand people were outside when the official communiqué was hung on the palace railings. But the crowd already knew, an official told a policeman 'It's a boy' and the policeman shouted the news to the crowd. They sang 'He's a Jolly Good Fellow' and chanted, 'we want Philip . . . we want Philip', but Philip did not want them. He wanted to stay with his family. There was no balcony appearance for the crowds that chilly November night.

Finally Mike Parker went to the Palace railings to try to disperse the shouting well-wishers as kindly as he possibly could. The people thought he was Prince Philip and more cheering broke out. He held up his hands, and looked for someone to talk to and to his astonishment found himself staring at David Niven.

It was Niven who was given the message that both the young Prince and his mother were doing well, and it was Niven who helped persuade the crowd to let the Princess get a good night's sleep.

And Philip's cup was full when in the autumn of 1949 the King's health recovered sufficiently for him to return to sea. He was made First Lieutenant and second-in-command of HMS *Chequers*, the leading ship in the 1st Mediterranean Destroyer Flotilla. She was based at Malta and his basic pay was £1.6s a day, plus allowances, making around £15 a week. The crew was ordered that there was to be no leg-pulling, his title was not to be mentioned and there was to be no publicity. But the good news was that it was decided that it would be possible for his wife to join him.

Christmas 1949 was the most different Christmas that Princess Elizabeth had ever spent. Instead of freezing Sandringham, she was in the warmth of Malta, living in Lord Mountbatten's house, the Villa Guardamangia, overlooking the harbour at Pieta. Lord Mountbatten was Flag-Officer Commanding the 1st Cruiser Squadron in the Mediterranean, and once again in a position to smooth things for his nephew.

The time that she spent in Malta was the nearest that the Queen has ever been to an ordinary, everyday existence. With Prince Charles left at home—the Establishment felt that the conditions in Malta were not suitable for him—she lived the life of a navy wife, going to the hairdressers in Valetta; watching her husband learn to play polo on the polo pony she had bought him for Christmas, and coached by Uncle Dickie. She perhaps was not like other naval wives, since she had Margaret 'Bobo' MacDonald, her personal maid, and Pearce, her footman, with her. Bobo had been with the Princess since she was a year old; they had never been separated, and now she was still always at her 'little lady's' side, much to Prince Philip's annoyance. He believed that Bobo had far too much influence on the Princess and that their relationship was too close. In turn, Bobo did not think he was anywhere near good enough for her little lady. They disliked each other and still do.

Princess Anne was conceived in the romantic atmosphere of Malta where the young couple had swum, sunbathed and gone dancing at the hotel Phoenicia. In the Spring of 1950 Elizabeth returned home to Clarence House and Philip flew home in time for the birth of their baby daughter. She was born on 15 August, and on that same day Prince Philip achieved his life-long ambition. He was gazetteered a Lieutenant-Commander and given the command of a ship of his own, HMS *Magpie*. Once Elizabeth had finished nursing Princess Anne she rejoined him in Malta.

Philip was working his crew hard for his frigate to be the cock ship of the fleet. Fiercely competitive, he wanted to be first at everything.

One of his ratings said: 'He worked us like dogs and treated us like gentleman.' They could expect a mouthful of what was primly called 'very strong language' in those days, but the men respected him because he asked them to do nothing that he would not do himself. In the annual regatta, his ship won six of the ten boat events, and he himself, stripped to the waist, rowing stroke, led one of the whalers to victory. And, crowing more than a little, he hoisted a huge red plywood cockerel on *Magpie* as proof that his was the cock ship of the 2nd Frigate Flotilla.

Magpie very soon became a floating embassy with ports of call around the Mediterranean. With his wife on board the C-in-C's despatch vessel, the larger and more comfortable *Surprise*, the Foreign Office decided that they could do a bit of 'flag-waving'. This flag-waving led to Princess Elizabeth's first visit to Greece where she met her husband's family on their own ground. It gave them a visit to Italy where they called on the President and were in trouble back home with extreme Protestants for a meeting with

101

the Pope. It also gave the Duke some glamorous shore leave in places like Monte Carlo.

He was 'kidnapped' by Italian university students who, when he was on a call into Venice, surrounded him in the piazza and gave him a mock trial before making him an honorary graduate. They accused him of having fair hair and invading the Doges' domain.

'I was allowed to defend myself,' Philip said, telling the story when receiving another honorary degree. 'I said I had fair hair because I was a descendant of the Vandals and Goths, and if it had not been for them there would not have been a settlement in Venice at all. As for invading the Doges' domain, I had merely come along to see how the settlement was getting on.'

He also paid formal calls on various Middle Eastern potentates, one of whom, President Jehal Bayar of Turkey gave him three more polo ponies.

The *Magpie* became known in the navy as Edinburgh's private yacht.

But the good times did not last. In less than two years Edinburgh had to say goodbye to his private yacht. The King's health was failing, the Princess Elizabeth was having to take over more and more of his work. She needed her husband's support. The Lieutenant-Commander was put on indefinite leave, his active service suspended. The two cars, one a Daimler, that he had kept on the island were shipped home. Michael Parker flew out to be with him for the last days, and they spent the last nights picnicking on quiet beaches, and fishing underwater, trying to cram the time with the pastimes that had given them the most pleasure. The Prince flew home on a Viking of the King's Flight reluctantly. For weeks he was moody and impatient. The game had not gone his way, and he was sulking, but he did get on with what was required of him.

And what was required of him was a tour of Canada and the United States. The intention had been to travel by sea, but the King was suffering from lung cancer and his health was so uncertain that the long sea voyage, with Elizabeth out of touch, seemed unwise.

It was then that Prince Philip made the first major step towards dragging the Establishment into the 20th century. He suggested that he and the Princess should fly. In 1951 it seemed a preposterous idea—on safety grounds—and was immediately rejected. Philip stuck to his guns, pointing out that if they did not fly, the tour would have to be cancelled. Reluctantly Clement Attlee gave his permission, and for the first time a royal couple used the air as an official means of transport across the Atlantic.

They came home in November after a successful tour. Occasionally not too well-chosen words from Philip had ruffled a few feathers, but basically the young couple had done a good job. On their return the King, to show his gratitude, created them both Privy Councillors. Another tour, to Australia and New Zealand, lay ahead for them. They were to leave at the end of January 1952.

The King saw them off at London Airport, standing on the tarmac, waving, hatless, his hair blowing in the cold wind. Their first stop was to be Nairobi where they carried out a few engagements. Then the Princess wanted to see Sagana Royal Lodge at Nyeri, their wedding present from the people of Kenya. From there, thoroughly enjoying themselves, they moved on to stay at the Treetops Hotel for a night before boarding the liner *Gothic* at Mombassa. It was a fascinating place, built into the branches of a vast wild fig tree and with a specially constructed platform for watching wildlife. It was there they spent the night, photographing the animals which came to drink at the waterhole below, before returning to the lodge the next day.

During that night Philip's life altered completely. While they were taking their photographs, the King died quietly in his sleep. Elizabeth succeeded to the throne.

Ignorant of the King's death, the young couple and their retinue returned to the Sagana Lodge where, after being up all night, they decided to have a rest. Word came through to the staff of the tragedy, but no official confirmation. Not until this confirmation came through, two hours later, was the Duke alerted by a shaken Mike Parker beckoning him through the window. Philip came outside to see what the matter was, and Parker said hesitantly: 'I'm afraid there's some awful news. The King is dead.' He then asked Philip if he would tell 'Her Majesty'.

It was the first time her new nomenclature had been used. A white-faced Prince Philip went back inside to tell his wife, the Queen, that her father was dead.

Michael Parker remarked afterwards that Prince Philip looked as if the weight of the world had descended on his shoulders when he heard the news. 'I never felt so sorry for anyone in my life,' he said.

It was the moment of truth for Prince Philip. The doors of the royal cage clanged shut. It was goodbye to his naval career, goodbye to any kind of informal life. It was the time to pay the price for the homes, the wealth and the life style and nothing would ever be the same again. HRH The Duke of Edinburgh was not a happy man.

8

PHILIP'S FUNNY FRIENDS

In the first years of his marriage, and when the silk-lined bonds of being the consort to the future Queen were beginning to chaff, Prince Philip began to run around with a group of men that his wife referred to as 'Philip's funny friends'.

Most of them he met through Mike Parker. Parker, court jester and confidant as well as equerry to the newly created HRH The Duke of Edinburgh, would sort out these people. They were mostly talented eccentrics whose life style was a million miles from that of the Palace and the Court; people he thought Philip would enjoy. And then he would effect introductions. He had an unerring instinct for finding people who would amuse the Prince and the unlikely companions he put into Philip's orbit were the light relief in the Prince's life for many years. Though the Establishment figures frowned and warned, Princess Elizabeth tolerated the friendships, but in the end, both Mike Parker and Philip's funny friends had to go.

Much of the problem was that Mike Parker's judgement of people was faulty. He, too, was attracted by talented eccentric oddballs and was curious to know those who veered towards being a touch sleazy. He—and Philip—enjoyed characters whose life style was not that of our own dear Queen! Therefore, against the advice of wiser counsel, like that of Lt General Sir Frederick 'Boy' Browning, who won the DSO at 19, the motley crew Parker gathered became part of Philip's set. They also became the subject of newspaper gossip. These were safety-valve people with whom the Prince could let down his hair.

105

Like others before him, he was seeking the company of fast people as a last desperate bid for an identity separate from the Monarchy before the royal cage door slammed shut on him. It was a futile attempt to keep the door ajar, and one that other princes have tried in the past, preferring, for a while, the company of the raffish to the refined. In this generation Prince Andrew has had his funny friends. Princess Diana now has hers, found through Fergie, who today plays the best-friend role in her life that Michael Parker once played in her father-in-law's. The irony is that today her father-in-law, once the worst offender of all, has little tolerance for his children's offbeat companions.

Parker himself was a man of considerable charm and ability, and like the Prince, young and wanting to fill his life with every experience. So personable was he that he quickly became as famous, as well-dressed, but considerably more urbane than his short-tempered master. He himself could have qualified as one of Philip's funny friends, yet the Princess was extremely fond of him and his gentle, Scottish wife.

He and Philip egged each other on. They were the closest of friends, enjoying the same pastimes, and in the early days of the Prince's marriage, when he and Elizabeth were living with the in-laws at the Palace, most of what they enjoyed was not particularly sophisticated.

In those days Philip loathed living at the Palace. He hated the formality of the place. He was also somewhat in awe of his tetchy father-in-law, the King. He found the servants, the service and the cossetted life style oppressive. The years have changed all that. The young Prince who snapped at the footman: 'I've got bloody hands, man!' when a door was opened for him, now expects his valet to put his toothpaste on his toothbrush. Night and morning.

But as a young man, he and Mike Parker between them tried to liven up the endless corridors and stuffy atmosphere of their enforced quarters. Parker brought a load of thunderflashes into Buckingham Palace, large ones that went off with a satisfying explosion. He and the Prince would set these off in the Palace until even the King felt himself obliged to complain and tell them to pack it in and stop frightening the servants.

They would have sliding competitions along the Palace corridors, running up to a mat, jumping on it and trying to keep upright until it slid to a halt. This, too, was frowned upon by the King after Mike Parker crashed into the King's study door. The mats would move, and fast, but there was no way of guiding them. Crashes were inevitable.

They called each other Murgatroyd and Winterbottom and if Murgatroyd and Winterbottom were going out for a stroll, it meant that they planned to slip out of the Palace together to spend an evening with like-minded mates. And there were occasions when they were out so late that the Palace was bolted and barred on their return. Royalty do not carry keys. In those days when security was not such a problem, they would help each other shin over the garden wall. They once managed to get themselves locked in the Palace swimming pool late one night, and only loud yells from Mike Parker got them released. All harmless stuff, and for a young man, missing his career, a relief from the pomp and circumstance of the life that he had chosen—yet chaffed against.

One of the first of the funny friends was Uffa Fox, a huge, gross man of enormous inventive talent. A sailor, a brilliant designer of yachts, a lover of the sea and ships, he and Philip became friends around 1948 when Michael Parker introduced them to Cowes Week. Uffa reigned over Cowes during that week and since the old buccaneer was not a man to be impressed by a title, Philip became part of *his* court. The future Queen's husband joined in noisy drunken parties—though never becoming remotely intoxicated himself. Hahn's Gordonstoun teaching against alcohol has made him a cautious drinker all his life.

There were never any women at Uffa Fox's parties. He had little interest in women, regarding them as useful only for cooking and cleaning. The young Princess Elizabeth was not invited to his Cowes Week parties nor, presumably, would she have wished to attend. It was unlikely that the gatherings in Uffa's Isle of Wight home would have been to her taste since the host enjoyed getting blind, noisy drunk—but only once every twelve hours. The only guests were groups of men, playing at being old salts, telling yarns, guffawing at dirty jokes and bellowing sea shanties while swilling red wine.

The parties were wild, but harmless. Silly rather than sinful and those who attended them sailed enthusiastically in competition as well. Philip had been given a small yacht, the *Bluebottle*, as a wedding present, and Uffa crewed for him along with two others.

Philip, at barely 30, had not lost his schoolboy humour. Jokes, like a motorhorn operated by a bulb placed under a cushion, were about the norm in pranks. Uffa and his friends thought that the long, mournful fart produced when the cushion was sat upon hilarious.

The London funny friends were most of a problem since their activities, nearer to the Palace, were more public. Most of the funny friends were found in the Thursday Club, a gathering of kindred spirits that met every Thursday at Wheelers in Old Compton Street, Soho.

Soho in those days had few strip clubs and clip joints. It was a pleasant London quarter where foreign restaurants were to be found. Not that Wheelers served foreign food. Their speciality was (and still is) fish, and in season the Thursday Club ate oysters and lobster claws washed down with a great deal of champagne and Guinness.

Again, these gatherings by modern standards were merely bawdy, noisy and rather drunken. Not unlike a modern day Hooray Henry's rugger-club outing. Lunch could stretch into the evening while wardroom jokes were told, dirty songs sung. Only one woman was ever present. Nancy Spain, the brilliant, but lesbian journalist, dressed as a man (her usual ensemble) once, and once only, crashed these male portals.

All members were allowed to bring one guest. This was the way the existing members vetted the prospective ones. And each month a Cunt of the Month was elected, the award going to the member who had either told the worst joke or made the biggest fool of himself over the past four weeks. It was perhaps a little *outré* for a man who was the husband of the Queen.

The membership, of whom few survive today, was mixed. Mountbatten's old adversary, *Daily Express* editor Arthur Christiansen belonged, as did politician Ian Macleod. There were two artist members, the raffish Vasco Lazzolo and the rumbustious Felix Topolski. Actors Peter Ustinov, James Robertson Justice and Michael Trubshawe were members. Anthony Beauchamp, one-time husband of Winston Churchill's daughter, Sarah, was keeper of the Club's records. These were a set of visitor's books filled with jokes and drawings that were strictly for their eyes only. When Beauchamp, a man whom his wife said was incapable of fidelity, died, they were passed to Lazzolo, who had a prediliction for young girls and prostitutes, but was nevertheless a man of humour rarely stuck for a come-back. When asked by a prospective lady client how much he charged for a half-length portrait, 'Which half?' he promptly enquired. His busts and paintings of Prince Philip were definitely of the top half.

Where are the visitor's books now? Alas, since Lazzolo's death they languish in a forgotten bank vault. Their bons mots and secrets may be lost for ever.

Many of the bons mots were contributed by American Larry Adler, the much-married harmonica player who joined the Club in 1947.

Adler, who unlike most of the other members is still with us, considered himself the wit of the Thursday Club. Example of the style of humour—the flamboyant James Robertson Justice defending the British public school system: 'I was buggered in my first week at Eton and it never did me any harm.'

Adler: 'Everyone had to watch you, I suppose, so that Justice was not only done but seen to be done.'

Adler was living in England after having been blacklisted by Senator McCarthy. He was a victim of the American witchhunts against left-wing thinkers of the fifties. As a result his work in America had dried up.

'In general, of course,' he says, 'the Thursday Club was right wing. I was the token red, and they always changed whitebait to redbait on the menu in my honour.

'The lunches were all-male occasions and Prince Philip, who came to many of them, arrived on time like everyone else. I never saw any security around him and everyone called him Philip. We never used his title.

'He was an agreeable man who made good jokes and was also a good audience. He seemed absolutely relaxed when he was with us and able to really let his hair down and enjoy himself. I never heard him once mention his family, the Queen or any of his royal duties.

'On one lunch date I remember we'd had a particularly good time and didn't want to call it a day so I invited everyone to come back to my flat in Grosvenor Square. Unfortunately I had not told my wife about this, and she opened the door wearing a bandana and clutching a hoover and duster to see Prince Philip and the Marquis of Milford Haven standing there. She was not amused.'

Adler remembers three particular occasions when Philip was at a Thursday Club meeting. The first was when Baron gave a 'sort of a stag evening' for the Prince a couple of nights before he married Princess Elizabeth. 'He looked,' said Adler, 'absolutely terrified.'

'Another time, he and his great pal, the Marquis of Milford Haven threw smoke bombs into the fireplace in our room. It was a deliberate prank on their part to stop another of our members, Baron, the photographer, winning a bet to shoot the cuckoo as it popped out of the cuckoo clock at three o'clock.

'The bombs caused a loud explosion and the room filled with smoke and then the police rushed in. Everyone was dashing about looking like a well-dressed version of the Black-and-White Minstrel Show.

'But the oddest thing of all was when Prince Bernhard of the Netherlands came as a special guest of the club to one of our dinners. When Bernhard was leaving, Prince Philip knelt down on the floor, made a lavish bow and said: 'Give my regards to her Imperial Majesty.' I thought that strange and significant in some way.'

Significant, indeed. Prince Bernhard, too, was consort to his wife, Queen Juliana. He and Philip both shared the same predicament of being number two, constitutionally not existing and having to live two paces behind their wives. It was a private joke between two men, forced to bow to their wives.

The Thursday Club lunches almost invariably ran on throughout the day. And Princess Elizabeth was by no means the only wife to be wondering where her husband was most Thursday evenings. On one occasion Michael Parker invited everyone back to his place, where to their surprise a woman swept in. She was Maria Callas, accompanied by Aristotle Onassis. Michael Parker, apart from being Prince Philip's private secretary, also represented Lockheed Aircraft Company and he was trying to sell Onassis a jet!

The keenest member of the Club and the founder was Baron, a society photographer who was to become another of Prince Philip's great friends. He had a withered arm which caused him to crouch in a crablike manner when photographing and which gave him a somewhat sinister appearance. Philip had met Baron through Uncle Dickie who had also wangled Baron the job of Court photographer. His full name was Baron Nahum, and he was the son of a Jewish immigrant from Tripoli who had been brought up as a middle-class lad in Manchester. A chance meeting with Louis Mountbatten in 1935 in Malta was to change his life. Through Mountbatten he was invited to take pictures of the Duke and Duchess of Kent and their children. He took the wedding pictures of Philip and Elizabeth, and he and the Prince had become friends. He was a very good photographer and Prince Philip who was, and still is, a respector of talent, liked him.

Baron and Philip were on the organizing committee of the Thursday Club and the Prince was therefore a regular dinner-guest at Baron's home. Baron was famous for his intimate dinner parties, but unfortunately, the photographer had other friends and other tastes. Most of his dinner parties—and the larger parties that he held at his studio—were normal enough. At other, less publicized, gatherings anything went sexually and between sexes. 'Men with men and women with women, as one invitee put it. Girls appeared bizzarely dressed only in masonic aprons. These parties were neither chic nor respectable and were kept very secret. As Eileen Parker says in her book, *Step Aside for Royalty*, Baron was no model of sexual propriety, and therefore it seems unlikely that the Prince would have been unwise enough to permit his presence to grace these secondary parties. Others of the Thursday Club certainly did attend.

Baron had less salubrious friends who were regulars at his questionable gatherings. One was Stephen Ward, the key figure in the Profumo affair. He was, apart from being an osteopath and an artist, a reasonably discreet procurer of ladies for his rich and famous clientèle until he came unstuck in 1963. His cover was blown by the antics of Christine Keeler and Mandy Rice Davies. He, like Baron, gave parties, but his were generally unabashed orgies, and since he never had any money, the guests had to bring their own bottle. In his memoirs, written before he committed suicide in 1963, he mentioned that Prince Philip had once, if not twice, been his guest. He remembered him 'with a very attractive girl called Mitzi Taylor.'

David, Marquis of Milford Haven, Philip's own cousin, boyhood friend and best man, was a regular at these gatherings. The third Marquis was a remarkably handsome man, once dubbed the world's most eligible bachelor. He had a fine war record. He was twice decorated for his courage in World War II destroyers — receiving the OBE in 1942 and the DSC and a mention in dispatches the following year. But as an adult he changed a lot from the naughty-boy teenage companion who climbed the roofs of Kensington Palace with an equally youthful Prince Philip.

In London society in the late forties and fifties, Milford Haven became dubbed 'the fun-loving Marquis', a euphemism in those days for a man for whom anything went. His looks may have been attractive; his personality was not. He had a lavatorial sense of humour, a morbid interest in sex, and could be arrogant and cold. Of all Philip's funny friends, in spite of being one of the family, he was probably the most unsuitable.

He, too, was a nephew of Lord Mountbatten, and the ambitious Lord is reputed to have said to him: 'If you marry Princess Margaret, then we'll have got the pair of them.'

For a while, Milford Haven's name was indeed linked with Princess Margaret, but his tastes in women were more exotic, and in any event the Princess was interested elsewhere. He married, by an extraordinary coincidence, an American divorcée — a Mrs Simpson, just as the Duke of Windsor had. The Royal family did not appreciate the joke and appreciated it even less when the marriage ended in the Mexican divorce courts.

Thereafter he was better known for escorting London's most beautiful women to London's most expensive nightclubs, and also for a long and stormy affair with the actress, Eva Bartok. Though it has never been confirmed, he was almost certainly the father of her baby. Eva Bartok broke her spirit on his indifference and spoke bitterly of sexual usage after they parted.

But his friendship with Philip survived much. What it did not survive was the story that he sold to a newspaper about the Prince's wedding day under the heading of 'Prince Philip's Secret Stag Party'. For Philip betrayal to the press was the unforgiveable sin.

The royal family themselves had their doubts about Philip's chosen companions. And indeed, in 1955 at the height of the drama when the Queen and Prince Philip opposed Princess Margaret's marriage to the divorced Peter Townsend, Princess Margaret struck back. She told the Queen the prevailing rumours. She spat out the stories of what went on in Baron's studio, what the Thursday Club did—were their frolics really so harmless?—and repeated a rumour that the Prince had been involved in a car accident when driving an unnamed woman.

The Queen refused to believe anything that was said, and was furious with her sister for listening to and repeating what she felt was slanderous gossip.

But not only Princess Margaret had her suspicions. Eileen Parker, wife of Michael Parker, remembers sharing a car with Princess Alexandra when they had been to a dance at the Dorchester. The Princess asked Mrs Parker what she thought of Philip's friends, some of whom had been present at the ball. Mrs Parker voiced her doubts, and the Princess agreed that a few of them were 'distinctly odd'.

Eileen Parker, like Rosemary Townsend, wife to Peter Townsend, was a casualty of the perils of working for royalty. Rosemary Townsend, lonely and neglected, had found another man. Even the most stalwart could break in royal service, 'Boy' Browning, Elizabeth's comptroller, took to the bottle under the pressure. In 1958 his wife, the author, Daphne du Maurier suggested to the Prince that if it would help she would leave her beloved home, Menabilly, in Cornwall, to live with him in London. He did, in fact, resign in 1959. But basically, as Eileen Parker found out, wives were a nuisance in Philip's masculine world.

She and Michael had been so in love, so proud of their two

babies, but as time went on there was no room in her husband's life for anything except his job and his duty to the Prince.

The marriage was falling apart at the seams just at the time when a royal tour of Australia was being planned in 1953. The Queen and Philip would be away for six months, and that meant that Michael Parker would be away for six months also.

Eileen Parker begged to be allowed to go with him. She was convinced that the marriage would not stand the strain of the parting. Reluctantly he agreed. In retrospect she would have been wiser to have stayed at home. By going on the tour, however little she tried to be involved with it, she had broken the unwritten rule that there is no place for wives in royal service. The only husband and wife act in the Palace is that between Prince Philip and the Queen.

One day at the races in Australia, Philip accidently bumped into her as he turned to attract someone's attention.

'What, you again?' he said. 'Everywhere we go you seem to turn up. You're getting like a piece of furniture around here.'

She was hurt and upset, and felt her eyes filling with tears. Her husband overheard the remark and tried to console her, but basically she had to battle with her feelings of rejection alone.

She wrote later: 'At no point, so far as I can see, did Prince Philip attempt to intervene in the gradual deterioration of Mike's marriage, though I suspect he knew. There was no attempt whatsoever at lessening Mike's workload, nothing that might have contributed towards a conciliation.'

Though, as Eileen Parker said, her husband's attitude was largely to blame in that he simply didn't want to work less. He loved his work and lived for it. But there was another factor involved. She was certain that he was having an affair. Some nights he did not come home, and there were never any explanations. If she wanted to know where he was, she had to ring the Palace secretaries. Once Prince Philip rang her, asking where Mike was.

'I don't know,' she replied, 'I thought he was with you.'

'Oh, no,' said Prince Philip, laughing and not bothering with the comfort of a white lie. 'He's got the night off.'

He then apologized for disturbing her and rang off.

On the return from the Commonwealth tour, Eileen asked her husband outright if he was having an affair. Astonishingly she was told that it was none of her business! It was then she realized there was nothing to do but divorce. Mike was agreeable, just so long as the royal family were kept out of it.

And then came the killer.

'Of course, you'll have to be in the wrong,' he said. 'My job comes first.'

These were the days when someone had to take the legal blame for a marriage breakup. Adultery was the usual grounds, but it was not done to cite the *real* person with whom the adultery had taken place. But evidence of adultery had to be given to the courts by a third party—usually proved by a hotel porter or maid.

The guilty party hired the 'other man or woman' for the night and hotels did a brisk business with men spending the night with some strange woman with generally nothing more erotic than a game of cards taking place.

None of this appealed to Mrs Parker. She was not the type to spend the night in an hotel room with a strange man, nor was she to blame. If anything was to blame, it was her husband's job. There was another aspect to consider. If she confessed to 'adultery' she could have lost custody of her two children. She declined to take the blame. Parker left the family home and moved into a borrowed flat in South Street, Mayfair and the divorce was put in motion.

There is no doubt that Philip was fully informed all the time about what was going on. Equally certain is that the Queen was kept in ignorance of Mike Parker's affair. In May of 1956, Parker wrote his boss a frantic letter, saying how he was trying to defend 'M', the lady with whom he was having an affair, his job and the Prince himself. As they had discussed, he was going to have to provide 'alternative and very cast-iron and very attractive evidence'. He was finding this painful, particularly as he could not tell 'M', a naval divorcée, born Marion Payne, whom he had met in Malta before her marriage broke up.

Worried about the effect on his job, Parker did consider cross-petitioning and fighting like hell, though on what grounds he did not say. But he had been assured by his lawyer that with the evidence of adultery, the case would be over in fifteen minutes and make no waves.

But before the divorce came to court, he had to occupy his mind with making plans for Prince Philip to open the Melbourne Olympics and they cooked up a scheme to go part of the way on the brand-new royal yacht, *Britannia*. They would be back at sea, their first and best love.

The idea developed into a round-the-world voyage, via the Antarctic, visiting the Galapagos Islands and the Falklands. This would give them the opportunity to see those red-for-British dots on the map which would normally be considered too small for a royal visit. They were to be accompanied by a motley collection of artists and naturalists. As Eileen Parker tartly put it: 'The funny friends were afloat,'

But Parker and Philip were elated at the thought of the trip. It was going to be just like the good old navy days all over again.

The trip covered nearly 40,000 miles in all and took four months. They set off in October and had to be back at Lisbon to meet the Queen for the British State visit to Portugal on 16 February. Philip was in no great hurry to get home. In the guise of good works, representing the Queen in her most farflung outposts he was thoroughly enjoying himself. And indeed, from a public-relations viewpoint the journey was a great success. Most of the places they visited had never been included on a royal tour and he received truly tumultuous welcomes. Parker was in no hurry to return home, either, not with divorce staring him in the face. His wife had filed her petition just before their journey began. They strung the voyage out as long as possible, even sailing on a research ship down through the Antarctic to see twelve of the research bases centred there. The Prince missed Christmas—but talked to his family on the radio telegraph from the Falklands. He missed his ninth wedding anniversary—but remembered to send the Queen white roses. He also missed the Suez Canal crisis and a change of ministry. But he did spot a reproduction painting of the Queen on a hotel wall in New Zealand and ask if he could have it to hang in his cabin.

They all had what you might call a lovely time. In Tristan da Cunha the locals built the Prince a beautifully decorated archway of welcome—and moved all the donkeys to the other side of the island in case they ate it!

The future President of the World Wildlife Fund went crocodile shooting and got one straight between its glowing cigarette-end eyes with one bullet. The six-foot length of handbag eventually arrived, tanned and cured, at Buckingham Palace to make goodies for the royal ladies.

There were mutterings back at the Palace about Philip's folly and it was hardly surprising that rumours of a rift in the marriage began to circulate. There wasn't any rift as such. The more likely truth is that the Queen agreed to the journey knowing that her husband was bored rigid with Court life, and that he was still bitter at the loss of his naval career. Her intention was quite possible to *prevent* a rift in the marriage before his discontent actually caused one. He was not happy, and never really has been, with Court life, though he has mellowed somewhat. But in those days he was still too young and energentic to be locked in the cage. And while he had all this excess energy, it would not be a bad idea to get him away from the funny friends, either.

But the trip was to end in tears. Eileen Parker had not intended to make public her divorce until her husband was back home and the voyage was over. She had instructed her solicitor to this effect, but for some reason, maybe financial, he chose to break her embargo and gave the story as a scoop to the Nigel Dempster of the day, Rex North of the *Sunday Pictorial*.

The news reached *Britannia* and the following day, Parker's solicitors issued a statement that said: 'We are authorized to state that Lt Commander Parker has tendered his resignation as Private Secretary to the Duke of Edinburgh and this has been accepted. The existing circumstances of his marriage make it impossible for him to carry on with his present occupation.'

Parker left Britannia and flew back to London on 6 February.

'Parker of the Palace Quits', 'Grim Duke sees off his friend, Parker' said the headlines. 'The Duke's Friend in Sensation'.

The curious thing was that both the Queen, by radio telephone, and the Duke urged him to stay. Not to do so, was undoubtedly his own decision. Much to Philip's truly deep dismay, he insisted on resigning. The *Britannia* headed for home with an embittered

Philip aboard, already missing his friend and feeling that Mike Parker had been thrown to the journalistic wolves. Once again he managed to convince himself it was all the fault of the Press. Mike Parker was more anxious that Philip's knowledge and connivance in Parker's extra-marital activities would become known.

But worse was to follow. As *Britannia* lay at harbour in Gibraltar, the London correspondent of the *Baltimore Sun* sent a dispatch to her newspaper, repeating the café-society gossip that there was a rift between Philip and the Queen. Perhaps unwisely this inspired Sir Michael Adeane to issue a statement from the Palace that said: 'It is quite untrue that there is a rift between the Queen and the Duke of Edinburgh'.

The press had held back from printing the rumours of the rift, but Adeane's statement let them off the hook. Out came the Thursday Club stories, the Baron stories – though Baron had died some months before – the rumours that Philip had been sent away for his own good and to keep him out of trouble. And why, after all this time, wasn't he flying straight home to see the Queen instead of remaining in Gibraltar until she joined him? 'Fly Home Philip!' urged the *Daily Mirror* on 11 February. Philip did no such thing, but he was an angry man when the Queen joined him in Gibraltar.

At the Guildhall lunch, which always concluded a royal tour, Philip made sure that Mike Parker was present and sitting as near to him as possible. In his speech, he endeavoured to explain that long separation from his family.

'I believe,' he said, 'there are some things for which it is worthwhile making personal sacrifices, and I believe that the British Commonwealth is one of those things and I, for one, am prepared to sacrifice a good deal if by doing so, I can advance its well-being by even a small degree.'

Sacrifice? What sacrifice? one asks oneself. The Prince's hypocrisy was staggering. There was no sacrifice involved in the round-the-world jolly jaunt, and if anyone had been sacrificed it was Parker. Later, the Prince admitted: 'He had to go,' but the Queen did make him a member of the Royal Victorian Order which might or might not have been some consolation.

But why did he have to go? What did he fear might come out in

118

the divorce? Surely it must have been more than the fact that Philip was aware of his affair with Marion Payne? As Eileen Parker points out there had been a number of people in high places before him whose marriages had ended and who had continued with their careers—including the Prime Minister, Sir Anthony Eden.

'My first instinct was to blame sheer panic for Mike's abrupt decision,' she wrote, 'but then on reflection I started to wonder if his resignation was a smokescreen for something, or somebody else . . .

'The key witness in the divorce case was Mike's cook and part-time housekeeper Mrs Kyra Semil (stage name, Kyra Vance), a former opera star. The correspondent was named as Mrs Mary Alexandra Thompson, whose true identity was never revealed.

'On February 28th, 1958 I was granted my divorce from Lieutenant-Commander Michael Parker in a formal hearing that lasted only fifteen minutes. The case was uncontested. Mike was in Mexico at the time and Mrs Thompson did not come forward.'

Mrs Thompson was undoubtedly a paid correspondent covering for the mysterious Marion Foulkes, née Payne, whom Mike Parker was so determined to protect. And in so protecting, protect his royal master as well? Whatever the reason, he and Marion Payne never married.

When Michael Parker flew back to England, ten years had gone by since Prince Philip had asked him to become nanny and general factotum. There are those who say that the Prince misses his company even today.

Parker's departure was the end of an era. It was the end of the funny friends, and for Philip, the beginning of middle age.

9

CONSORT

Philip spent the first few months of the new Queen's reign in a state of black depression. His young wife was coping astonishingly well with her new responsibilities, the years of training guiding her through the morass of protocol and precedence. But her husband had not been trained from birth to face this total disruption to the very pleasant life style he had pieced together since their marriage.

Suddenly he was no one. Unimportant. He felt buried. His career was gone, and when he did try to involve himself in matters of state, he was smartly snubbed. The Establishment still did not trust him and his ambitious Mountbatten background. In the hierarchy he was listed as holding 'an office of profit under the Crown.' The office of profit was as husband to the Queen.

It was not an easy situation for a dominant man, who all his life had wanted to be out in front. One could argue that surely he must have realized that to be number two would be his future one day. But he had expected to take the back seat much much later. It would have been reasonable to bank on the King living until 70, which would have given him another thirteen years of fun. Assuredly in that time he would have become an Admiral of the Fleet by his own efforts, and not merely because he happened to be married to the Queen. He deserved to be an admiral and for a man of Philip's temperament, unearned honours meant little.

'I am just a lodger here,' he said despondently when they returned to Buckingham Palace. 'I am determined to be more than the Queen's husband.'

The Queen did her best for him, though she was and still is, far too duty-bound to veer from protocol. If her husband was not

120

officially meant to be present or involved at any one of her official engagements, she would not argue for him to be there—though he did push himself in on some occasions! Perhaps Elizabeth sensed that he could so easily swamp her, though she is stronger than she appears. Still, there were those in both the Government and the Court who preferred he did not have his finger in any official pies and made sure he had no chance to meddle.

In September 1952 the Queen issued a royal warrant which stated that: 'His Highness, Philip, Duke of Edinburgh, henceforth and all occasions shall have hold and enjoy Place, Preeminence, and Precedence next to her Majesty.'

In simpler terms, as an everyday illustration of the meaning of the warrant: she has no passport; his passport is numbered One, which just about sums it up.

Winston Churchill, Prime Minister of the day, insisted that they move back to Buckingham Palace. It was the official home of the Monarch and there they must be. Philip had to leave Clarence House, the home that he had created with so much pleasure and return to the endless corridors and the office atmosphere of the Palace. Windlesham went, too, swapped for the vastness of Windsor Castle as a weekend home. At the Palace they gave him a large ground-floor room since space was short. The Queen Mother, understandably, was in no hurry to move on. He brought his own bed and the huge television that had been a wedding present with him, but this modern-minded Prince found himself surrounded by heavy ornate furniture and portraits of long-dead foreign royalty, with his wife on the floor above.

It was hardly surprising that he went down with an attack of jaundice.

About the only consolation was that Parliament increased his state allowance to £40,000 a year. And the other, that the swimming pool led straight off his bedroom in the Belgium suite.

Many things irritated him. He could not bear the piper who every morning at breakfast time played beneath the Queen's window. He once said sourly: 'I think I've heard this song before. Sometimes they play it in tune, other times they play it out of tune.' He hated the fact that no one could see him or talk to him without making an appointment through his page. He thought there were too many staff and used much energy trying to cut down the number, only for them to grow, like a Hydra head, back to their original strength.

Remembering his impatience and bad temper of those days, it is interesting to see how the Palace system beat him. He probably no longer even hears the pipe major who still plays every morning because the Queen likes him to do so. He has discovered that the system of appointments through his page can save him an awful lot of unwanted visitors. And though he would once shout at footmen for opening doors for him, today they would probably get a blast if they didn't.

Cured of his jaundice, which was perhaps psychological as much as anything else, and after some miserable and depressed weeks in bed in the gloomy room, he decided to learn to fly. A decision that was much against the wishes of Winston Churchill. But since Philip's rank as Consort meant that he must become a courtesy Marshall of the Royal Air Force (*and* and Admiral of the Fleet *and* a Field Marshall), he could not bring himself to accept the title without being able to pilot a plane. He received his wings on 4 May 1953 . . . a month before the Queen received her crown.

The Coronation had not even taken place, when Lord Mountbatten precipitated another blow for his nephew. Uncle Dickie was busy pointing out that since 7 February 1952, a Mountbatten (if only by marriage) had sat on the throne. Queen Mary was outraged. Her husband, George V, had founded the House of Windsor, and no Battenberg/Mountbatten marriage could change that. In a fury she sent a message to Winston Churchill about Uncle Dickie's boasts. Churchill was equally outraged. He called a cabinet meeting and it was decided then and there that the Queen should be advised that the name of the royal house was the House of Windsor.

The Queen had no choice other than to wipe her husband's name from the family tree. She made the declaration that was demanded of her. Philip was briefly furious and then resigned to it. He hadn't been too keen on taking the name in the first place, and Uncle Dickie *was* tiresome and embarrassing. Philip was already beginning to resent Mountbatten's constant efforts to

(left) The beautiful Queen Alexandra of Yugoslavia, in 1943. Before her marriage, she, too was a Princess of Greece and one of Prince Philip's closest women friends. The picture, taken by Cecil Beaton, is signed for "Mougey"—her mother, Queen Aspasia of Greece.

(below) Helene Cordet and her two children, Max and Louise. It is 1955, and she is returning from a cabaret tour in Canada. Max and Louise, both godchildren of Prince Philip are meeting her from the boat-train.

JAN. 16, 1957
TWO SHILLINGS

MRS RONALD FERGUSON

(opposite) Monarch of all he surveys. The happy times when the King was alive and well, and Prince Philip was in charge of his own ship the HMS *Magpie* and on the summer Mediterranean cruise. His critics referred to the *Magpie* as Edinburgh's private yacht.

(above) The attractive Susie Ferguson, mother of the Duchess of York, gracing the cover of the Tatler in the days when she and Prince Philip were close friends. She is now married to Argentinian polo player Hector Barrantes.

(right) Pat Kirkwood, the West End superstar of the forties, fifties and sixties who took Prince Philip's fancy for just one glamorous night of dancing. The evening at the swish Les Ambassadeurs Club led to rumours that she was his girl-friend, rumours that still persist today.

(above) A Baron photograph taken just prior to the death of King George VI, 1952.

(opposite above) One of the most informal pictures ever taken of Prince Philip. He is playing with photographer Baron's cat, in Baron's flat, while his friend and equerry, Michael Parker, checks the engagement diary. Baron said it was one of the Prince's favourite photographs.

(opposite below) Enjoying a laugh at a London nightclub are (left to right) Frank Sinatra, Ava Gardner, Mrs C.J. Latta, Prince Philip and Dorothy Kineton.

(above) The Queen's 42nd birthday in 1968. Prince Philip's family is complete in this official birthday photograph, but all his offspring seem to be showing their father's distaste for the camera.

(opposite top left) It was Uncle Dickie who taught Prince Philip to play polo when they were both stationed in Malta in 1949. The Queen bought him his first polo pony for Christmas that year.

(opposite top right) By 1956, Prince Philip had turned a section of Great Windsor Park into a polo field. This June day, the Queen with Prince Charles and Princess Anne went to watch him play.

(opposite below) Sailing with the 'funny friends'. Prince Philip with Uffa Fox (centre) on Coweslip (a wedding present) at the Cowes Regatta.

(left) Throughout his married life, Prince Philip has made secret trips to visit his German relations on their Estates. Here he is photographed with his brother-in-law, Berthold, after a wild boar hunt at Zwingenberg in 1959.

(below) Great Windsor Park, 1983. Prince Philip welcomes his second cousin, Princess Alexandra, into his landrover.

appear that he alone had been Philip's protégé. It was something that never stopped. Even a few months before his horrendous death in 1979, Mountbatten said complacently to a journalist: 'He [Philip] can be a little offhand with me sometimes but I think I brought him up on the right lines.'

Since Philip was 17 before Uncle Dickie came on the scene, he had had little to do with bringing up his nephew on the right lines or otherwise.

But he and the Queen weathered the storm, and anyway, it was all put right again eight years later.

The Establishment gave way sufficiently to make him chairman of the Coronation Committee. However, since in thirty days he managed to keep up his flying lessons, play twenty games of polo and accompany the Queen on seventy-six engagements, not surprisingly most of the work was done by the Duke of Norfolk. Though, being the workaholic that he is his contribution was considerable.

His role in the Coronation was to kneel before his wife, taking the ancient oath of fealty . . . 'I, Philip, Duke of Edinburgh, do become your liege man of life and limb and of earthly worship; and faith and truth will I bear unto you, to live and die, against all manner of folks. So help me God.' He then had to stand, kiss her cheek and back away. At the rehearsal, probably feeling a bit of a chump, he did not play his part with any conviction. In fact, he sent it up, mumbling the words at high speed, missed the Queen's cheek and retired backwards fast. The Queen showed her mettle by saying indulgently: 'Don't be silly, Philip. Come back here and do it properly.' He performed more seriously on the day, but his touch on the huge crown was a little heavy handed. The Queen had to put it straight.

And within weeks of the Coronation, he and Elizabeth had to deal with what was probably the biggest crisis of her reign.

It was a simple little gesture that sparked off what was to become the scandal of the decade.

Outside the Abbey, after the ceremony, the guests waited for their coaches to take them back to the Palace. Princess Margaret was with them, standing laughing and animated at the side of the slight figure of Group Captain Peter Townsend. Townsend, who had served the King since 1944, was as close to the royal family as a son, and on the King's death, the Queen Mother had made him comptroller of her new household.

Princess Margaret was just a little too close to him, and laughing, she picked a stray thread from the pocket of his uniform, and then brushed her hand along the row of medals on his chest. It did not go unnoticed by the Press, and the affectionate little touch on the uniform of the man she loved unleashed a flood of specualtion.

As if the Queen and Philip did not have enough on their minds, a few week's before the Coronation, Princess Margaret had told her mother and sister that she wanted to marry Townsend. He was sixteen years older than her, but the real problem was that he was a divorced man, although admittedly the innocent party. He had watched Margaret grow up since the age of 14, and what had started as a schoolgirl crush for the blue-eyed, romantic wavy haired Battle of Britain pilot, had developed into real love.

The Queen herself was very fond of him. As her father's equerry he had been part of their lives for a long time. He and Philip were not so close. Townsend was well established in the Palace in 1946 when Prince Philip came on the scene. Townsend was a hero in a younger service and he was also a romantic, something of an intellectual, interested in poetry and art, and never said or did anything contentious or unkind. He had little in common with the abrasive Duke and he seemed to bring out all the Philip's competitiveness. They fought each other with the ferocity of two stags on the squash courts, and the word was that Townsend had sided with the King when the King insisted on delaying Philip and Elizabeth's engagement.

This could well be true, since Townsend himself had experience of rushing into what for him was a disastrous marriage. Certainly when Philip was invited to Balmoral to be looked-over by the King, Townsend was another watcher, and it is said that it was Townsend who suggested that he be invited for this purpose. Writer Willi Frischauer in his biography of Princess Margaret said that hearing this, Prince Philip was furious: 'What a cheek,' he said, 'for a man who was already heading for a break-up with his wife to set himself up as a marriage counsellor!'

Peter Townsend himself says he had no hand in any of it.

Today he lives in Paris with his second wife, a Belgian woman who is half his age and he says: 'I was not against Philip's marriage to the Queen. I've never told anyone who they should or should not marry. I wouldn't even interfere with my own sons.

'I was prepared to like Philip. I knew of him first through my brother Michael who was captain of a destroyer in the war. Philip sailed under him and later, when Philip became a pilot, my admiration for him increased because of my own love for flying.

'The one thing we did do was fight battles against each other on the courts. Badminton and squash. Philip would fight me to a standstill. He wanted to win every time. One time he was so intent on the game that he nearly broke my wrist. And when I went into exile in 1953, he did not exactly walk me to the door and say goodbye, though we had known each other for many years and had dined together with the Queen and Margaret.

'During those times that we were together he was always polite and friendly. Never imperious. He is a German but he does not look very German. He is certainly trenchant and his views are trenchant. I would say he is intelligent without being an intellectual.

'When I was there he could be abrupt and he has this staccato way of talking, although he will often end things up with a joke or a quip.'

Peter Townsend might have been 'prepared to like him'—but did he? And he had suffered from the Prince's quips when Philip saw fit to make jokes about his affair with Margaret. In his book, Peter Townsend says that he was impressed 'by the Queen's movingly simple and sympathetic acceptance of the disturbing facts of her sister's love for me . . . Prince Philip, as was his way, may have tended to look for a funny side to this poignant situation. I did not blame him. A laugh here and there did not come amiss.'

Even all these years later, it is a cautious and careful assessment from a discreet man who wishes to harm no one. There is no great warmth in his judgement of the Duke, but that is hardly surprising. There may be doubt that Townsend involved himself in Philip's affairs, there is no doubt that Philip involved himself in Townsend's.

Under the Royal Marriages Act of 1772, the Queen had to put her sister's request to Winston Churchill. She had to act on the advice of her Prime Minister. Churchill considered that to say yes would be a disasterous start to the reign, and he suggested that the couple wait for two years. By then Princess Margaret would be 25, and again under the rules of the marriage act, free to make her own decision. He also felt that Townsend should be removed from Clarence House, and so did Prince Philip.

The Queen would not have it. She could not bear to separate her sister from the man she loved. It was decided that Townsend would stay, and that things would be allowed to drift on, though there would be no engagement. Prince Philip was not happy with the decision. He felt even the possibility of the marriage could diminish and threaten the dignity of the crown.

Margaret's loving gesture blew the gaff! The royal family had a full scale scandal on their hands. At Churchill's insistence, Townsend, with the Press baying at his heels, was sent away for a year to Brussels as Air Attaché while Margaret went to Southern Rhodesia with her mother. It must have been a lonely trip for her. Peter Townsend had originally been intended to accompany them.

The problem did not go away. When in 1955, Margaret became 25, she was still insistent that she wanted to marry Townsend and was quite free to do so—if she gave up all her royal rights. Peter Townsend came home and he and Margaret met again at the home of the Queen's friends, Mr and Mrs John Lycett Wills who found themselves in a state of siege with the world's Press camped around their mansion.

Sir Anthony Eden, the new Prime Minister, made it clear that if the marriage did take place, the Princess would have to leave the country. And Prince Philip was totally opposed to the marriage. He scuttled it at a private dinner party at Windsor attended only by the Queen, the Princess and Philip himself. Philip was adamant. There could be no marriage. It was out of the question. Such a union would bring disrepute to the Monarchy, offend the Church and the public. Margaret must stop this stupidity immediately.

Margaret telephoned Townsend the next day and cried as she told him that the situation looked hopeless. They arranged to meet at Clarence House, and that night he sat up writing the words with which the Princess renounced her love. They met for the last time at Clarence House, and an hour later the words he had written were broadcast.

'I would like it to be known that I have decided not to marry Group Captain Townsend. I have been aware that, subject to my renouncing my rights of succession, it might have been possible for me to contract a civil marriage. But mindful of the Church's teaching that Christian marriage is indissoluble, and conscious of my duty to the Commonwealth, I have resolved to put these considerations before others. I have reached this decision entirely alone, and in doing so I have been strengthened by the unfailing support and devotion of Group Captain Townsend. I am deeply grateful for the concern of all those who have constantly prayed for my happiness.'

It took time for wounds to heal, and the atmosphere between Philip and Margaret has never totally recovered. But then he never had much sympathy for her, finding her vain and frivolous. Today she still irritates him and, in many cases, the mischievous Margaret irritates him quite deliberately.

And who can blame her.

10

PHILIP THE FATHER

On his desk at Kensington Palace, just after his marriage, Prince Charles kept a photograph of himself and his father. It pictured them both dressed in Trinity House (the lighthouse institution) uniforms with the Prince of Wales one step behind his father, but in the same stance—hand on sword. On the photograph Prince Charles has written: 'I was not made to follow in my father's footsteps.'

A small protest against the sometimes overbearing attitudes of his father? Or just a joking reference to the fact that he was born to follow in his mother's footsteps? Who knows. Perhaps a mixture of the two.

Philip has always had the strongest say in the upbringing of the children. It has been a long running responsibility. He was 26 when his first son was born in the first year of his marriage. He was 43 when his last son, Edward, was born, and had been married for seventeen years. It was he who made the decisions about their schooling—his are the first British royal children to go to school. And the boys went to his old schools, Cheam and Gordonstoun. The Prince was particularly keen that Charles went to Gordonstoun so that he would get the chance to mix and be toughened up. On this he overruled the Queen who would have much preferred that Charles went to the more traditional Eton. She preferred Eton mainly because it was convenient to Windsor Castle where the royal family spend most weekends. She may also have thought that it would be simpler for Charles since he would meet the children of their friends there. But Philip got his way. As he usually does.

Prince Charles is most unlikely to follow in his father's footsteps simply because it would not be possible for him to do so. He does not have the temperament, though heaven knows he has tried to live up to everything that his father expected of him. But he is not by nature competitive, nor is he aggressive. Where his father is abrasive, Charles is anxious to bruise no feelings. 'Prince Philip has many qualities,' said one who knew him well, 'but sensitivity is not among them.' His eldest son is both sensitive and thoughtful.

Prince Philip himself said that: 'Charles has his mother's serenity and concern for individuals, but also her unsuspected inner toughness.' He went on to add that: 'Anne has a lot of my own abrupt directness and practicality.'

For a man of Charles's temperament, Prince Philip is a difficult father to live with. Indeed, all three of his sons have found his hand on them heavy at times as they grew older. His daughter, Anne, who is the most like him, has no problems. They understand each other very well.

Charles as the eldest has always had the most difficulties. Though he adored and hero-worshipped his 'papa' when he was a little boy there was an underlying terror of his father who had no patience with a gentle little boy. Philip was determined to make a man of his son, and at an early age Charles was driven three times a week to a private gymnasium in Pavilion Road, Chelsea, where a small class of boys was instructed in physical training and boxing. Prince Philip himself taught Charles and Anne to ride. He rode with them when they learned to canter, and he personally superintended their initiation into jumping their ponies. While the Queen was away at Sandringham, he taught them to jump in the grounds of Windsor Castle. He had had bales of straw put out on the lawn which was specially marked out for the occasion.

They were taught to swim by their father who started them with swimming exercises in the nursery, breast-stroking like mad while lying on their tummies on a pouffe. When they'd got the hang of it, they graduated to the shallow end of the Palace pool. He taught Charles to sail and shoot, and played bicycle polo with him. Charles had his own little miniature wooden mallet. At Balmoral he would take both Charles and Anne out in the

Landrover with sleeping bags and cooking equipment and spend the night in one of the many cabins on the Balmoral Estate. In all this he was still following the teachings of his mentor Kurt Hahn and his own schooling at Gordonstoun. He believed, and no doubt still believes, that if a child is self-confident in one area, it spills over into another.

It worried him in the early days of the marriage when he was still a serving naval officer and frequently away that Charles was completely surrounded by women, a petticoat government consisting of his mother, his nanny, his governess and his sister. Like most fathers, Philip did not want his son to be mollycoddled. He was determined on boarding school to put it all right.

He was a very good father despite being away a great deal when his first two children were small. When Charles and Anne were very little he did not think it unmanly to push them in their pram. And when they grew a little, still young himself, he joined them in games of football in the wide corridors of Windsor, showed them how to make sandcastles on the windy Norfolk beaches, and enjoyed a game of cowboys and Indians.

There was playtime every morning, and the children came down from the nursery just after 5 pm for another romp with their parents. At 6 pm, the Queen and her husband would take the children back to the nursery, and more often than not would stay for bathtime. Sometimes they would send the nursery maid away and bath the children themselves.

There were long separations from all four of their offspring when duty called, and the gap between the first two and the last two of the family was caused because the Queen could not possibly have taken time off for a pregnancy in those early days on the throne.

It was in 1956 when Philip first made his views on the education of the heir to the throne public.

'The Queen and I want Charles to go to school with other boys of his generation and learn to live with other children, and to absorb from childhood the discipline imposed by education and others,' he said.

There was no question of sending the little Prince to a State school, though there were those who urged it. Wisely the Prince ignored these suggestions, but succumbed to every dad's dream of sending his son to his own old school. Charles was sent to Cheam, and that was difficult enough for him. State school would have been a nightmare. As small as he was, he was doubtful about living away from home, but like many a small boy before him, he had no choice in the matter.

Charles turned out to be an average scholar. This caused him no problems at home. Not having been the greatest of scholars himself, his children's academic abilities have never worried Prince Philip. He once said that he'd prefer they weren't at the bottom of the class all the time, but somewhere around the middle would suit him fine.

In spite of the evidence, he himself does not accept that his views were imposed on his children or that he was a forceful father. 'It's no good saying do this, do that, don't do this, don't do that . . .' he has said. 'It's very easy when children want something to say no immediately. I think it's quite important not to give an unequivocal answer at once. Much better to think it over. Then, if you eventually say no, I think they really accept it.'

He told Basil Boothroyd, who wrote his informal biography, that the children were all encouraged to take their own line and argue it out.

'From the beginning,' he said, 'I was careful not to make a rigid plan—I haven't for any them—until some sort of foreseeable situation.'

He says he put the pros and cons of Gordonstoun against Eton to Charles himself, pointing out that Eton was too available to the Press, that Eton was often in the news, and that would reflect on Charles. He also pointed out that the north of Scotland was out of sight of the press, and that it wasn't far from Balmoral where he could always go and stay, and that his grandmother would be up there fishing and he could go and see her.

Not too many pros for Eton, one might say, from this old Gordonstoun pupil. Charles who was extremely close to his father at the time, did as he was subtly bid and went to Gordonstoun, where, at first he was thoroughly miserable. He made impossible plans to run away, but on receipt of a desperate letter from Charles his granny went up to Scotland to see him and gave him the courage to stick it out.

It is possible Philip never realized how unhappy his son was since he'd loved all the character-building, macho curriculum so much himself. He made a dramatic entrance once at the school to see his son, emerging from a helicopter, piloted by himself. Charles, like any schoolboy with a parent who goes a little over the top, could have died of embarrassment.

Since the hero-worshipping days, Charles and his father have grown apart. Philip is obsessed with being 'manly' and it is that macho part of his temperament that has caused problems between himself and his son. There was no way that he could turn Charles into a superman in spite of putting him through the refined masochism of Timbertops, the outback school in Australia, and Gordonstoun with its early morning runs and cold showers. Their tastes in so many things, big and small, are quite different. Charles likes to wallow in a bath, his father likes a quick bracing shower. Charles likes to discuss philosophy. Philip thinks it a load of codswallop. Charles likes opera and music, but a night at Covent Garden would drive his father to fling himself from the royal box. They are both interested in painting, but paint in a totally different style, Charles being the more traditional of the two. And their opinions can clash. On the Balmoral Estate there is a small, cosy house called Craigowan where Princess Diana and Prince Charles spent part of their honeymoon. The walls are decorated with Prince Philip's paintings, all in the abstract manner. Prince Charles does not care for this style of painting, and when he and the Princess stay at Craigowan his father's paintings are all moved to the staff rooms. The staff then put the original collection of highland paintings, and drawings of Queen Victoria and her family back where they were.

Stubbornly, Philip has his paintings replaced when he returns to the house for the pre-Christmas shoot which takes place every year. And so it goes on.

The Prince of Wales is also slower, less restless, than his father. While Philip, who has always had an enormous appetite, shovels food into his mouth to get the meal over as quickly as possible,

Charles likes to dawdle over his food. At formal dinners, no one must still be eating after the Queen. She gets around the problem for her guests by having a small salad to toy with until everyone has finished. Charles will be talking and playing with the food on his plate until suddenly he catches his father's baleful eye on him and hastily puts down his knife and fork.

Philip is also irritated by Charles when they are shooting. If Charles sees something that interests him, he will stop and look at it, momentarily distracted from the birds and the beaters. Even in front of guests, Prince Philip is liable to bawl at his son: 'Move your bloody arse!'

Charles takes little notice, and nor does anyone else. Philip always gets tetchy with anyone who holds up the shooting. When Princess Margaret was married to Anthony Armstrong-Jones, he, like everyone else, was obliged to join in the shooting parties. (Harold Wilson was one of the few to get out of it.) Though Armstrong-Jones is normally a good shot, he was having a bad day. Finally Philip turned and snapped at him: 'For God's sake Tony, why don't you shoot with your bloody camera? You might do better.'

So an outburst from papa on the grouse moors is not to be taken seriously.

Unfortunately, Charles' temperament makes him easy to bully, and therefore, right up until the time he married, Philip frequently bullied him, and bullied him hard enough to cause real distress.

The deep and basic difference between Philip and his eldest son showed itself at the death of Lord Louis Mountbatten. In later years Philip had not been so close to his Uncle Dickie as in the past, but Mountbatten had become Charles's guru. If Prince Charles had a problem he took it to Dickie Mountbatten. He called him his honorary grandfather and he was Mountbatten's honorary grandson. His appalling death at the hands of the IRA shattered Charles. He was torn by grief.

A few days after the assassination, Prince Philip, Prince Charles, with Lord Rupert Neville, Prince Philip's treasurer and private secretary, went down to Mountbatten's home, Broadlands. They were to have lunch there before going on to Lydd

Airport to receive Lord Mountbatten's body after it was flown back from Ireland.

John Barrett, Lord Mountbatten's private secretary, was also at the lunch and it was a sorrowful occasion with little said. Prince Charles was so grieved that he could barely speak. Prince Philip was masking his own loss with a brusque and abrupt manner. Just before lunch was served, Prince Charles slipped away and went down to the River Test where he used to fish when he stayed with his Great Uncle Dickie. It was one of his favourite places, and he stood there watching the water and composing himself for what lay ahead.

When his absence caused lunch to be delayed, his father became irritated and sent John Barrett to fetch him back. When Barrett saw the Prince standing there, head bowed, desolate, he could not bring himself to disturb him. He turned back without doing or saying anything and told Philip that his son would be back shortly.

When Charles did sit down to lunch, presumably trying to stiffen his backbone, Prince Philip embarked on a course of baiting his son. Eventually the Prince of Wales rose and quietly left the table, his dignity intact.

The cracks between them started to appear well before Prince Charles married. Philip had been pressurizing his son to find a girl, settle down and marry. He kept grumbling that if Charles, at the age of 32 didn't hurry up there wouldn't be anyone suitable left. When Charles did find someone suitable, Lady Diana Spencer, it took him a long time to make up his mind. Again the Duke began pressurizing his son, worried that it could appear that Charles was dallying with such a young girl. But he was delighted and content once Charles announced his engagement and their relationship returned to normal for a period.

It began to degenerate again 1984 when it seemed that Philip believed that marriage to Diana was softening up the son he had worked so diligently to toughen. No great thinker himself he was deeply suspicious of Charles' fascination with mystics like Laurens van der Post. Van der Post taught Charles about the natural way of life and opened up his mind to something deeper than winning at games. No acolyte of Kurt Hahn could be expected to understand, and Prince Philip did not. He did not see that as an adult married man, with his own children, Prince Charles no longer had to strain to be someone that he was not in order to please his father. He was able to be himself and give free rein to his own interests. If these included vegetarianism and having a look at the Kalahari tribesmen and his father did not approve – so be it.

Philip was also angry, and with justification, that Charles was not pulling his weight. It had been agreed that the engagements would be cut down while the children were small, but not to the extent that Charles and Diana had wangled for themselves. After the birth of Prince Harry, they only agreed to a dozen engagements in a four month period. Prince Philip, whose engagement book is always full and who believes that a blank or so in its pages is an offence, felt they were putting a strain on the rest of the family. Which they probably were.

He showed his displeasure by not flying down from Balmoral to see his new grandson when Harry was born. He stayed in Scotland for three more days of practice for the National Carriage Driving Championships. He had built an obstacle course on the golf course at Balmoral, and working on the theory that all babies look the same, wasn't going to waste it.

It was five weeks before the new baby received a visit from his grandfather.

And yet those who know him say that Philip has always believed in a strong and united family. He is convinced that the family unit is a protection against outside influences and that without it, it is possible to be influenced by the wrong things and the wrong people.

These are his fears for the independent Charles. For some time Philip has been concerned at his son's choice of confidant. It seems obvious that Charles is trying to fill the void left by the death of Lord Mountbatten with another elderly guru figure and his choices are perhaps offbeat. The friendship with Laurens van der Post puzzles Prince Philip but does not worry him. He is much more concerned by the friendship with Armand Hammer, the multi-millionaire, internationally powerful oil man. Hammer has homes in America, Moscow and London and though he has been photographed with the most powerful men in the world, the framed picture he keeps on his desk is one of his wife holding Prince William with Princess Diana beside him.

The Americans believe Hammer is a communist; the Russians think he is the only capitalist they can trust. Whatever he is, he has become Charles's confidant, and significantly Hammer has put up money for many of Charles's causes and interests. He has given money to the Royal Opera, to the Mary Rose Trust, and he even arranged the Neil Diamond concert for the Princess of Wales. He has given money to the United World Colleges of which Charles has been patron for many years. He is also always willing to send one of his airplanes if the Prince wants to take a quiet trip anywhere.

The relationship troubles Prince Philip because of what he calls 'the buying up' syndrome.

He has said that he will patronize a cause first, if he thinks it is right, then, after he has patronized it people may donate if they wish. What he won't have is people donating to one of his causes and then expecting his patronage, arguing that puts him the position whereby people believe they can buy his services. But Prince Charles doesn't appear to want to know about this viewpoint. Therefore, it is hard to see a reconciliation between father and son in the near future.

Philip has his favourite child—Princess Anne, and however badly and rudely she has behaved in public in the past, he always forgave her. One suspects he may well even have applauded her behaviour. For her brusqueness, impatience and visible hatred of the Press are his—along with the dedication to do a job well and see it through. She's gutsy, a worker, incredibly brave and not particularly imaginative—just like her dad. She has his good qualities as well as his bad, and he recognizes himself in her. She is a chip off the old block.

They rarely get the chance to talk privately away from the rest of the family, and because of that Philip often sends his daughter letters rather than trusting to the phone.

Once, at the height of the rumours when her personal detective, Peter Cross was dismissed for 'over familiarity', Philip sent his daughter a short note. In it he said he had heard what was being said and added simply: 'Please take care of yourself.'

He is her staunchest defender. In 1984 when there was speculation that her marriage was cracking, and the press put a lot of play on the fact that she and Mark Philips would sleep in separate hotels during the Los Angeles Olympics, it was to her father that she turned.

Mark Philips did stay downtown, not because the marriage was cracking, but to be with the people he was working with. Anne and her father shared a double suite in a uptown hotel and, putting up a united front, charmed the Americans—something neither of them make a habit of doing!

She is better on a horse than he is, and he was beside himself with pride when he watched her win £5 by completing a clear round at the Badminton Horse Trials while she was still a schoolgirl, pride that was repeated when, in July 1987, she won the Dresden Diamond Stakes at Ascot on Ten No Trumps. It came in at nine to one.

When she left school it was a bad time. She had few friends, no boyfriends and no idea of what she wanted to do. She was becoming a depressed and surly teenager. Philip realized that problem. He spoke to his polo-playing friends who had children of similar age. The invitations to parties flooded in, and Anne began to enjoy more of a normal teenage life.

In fact, what goes on between parents and children in the royal family is little different from the tensions and traumas of any family in the land. All fathers come the heavy hand at times and Prince Philip is no different. In the best regulated families there are also problems with the children, and the royal family have had their share of those, too.

Though Prince Philip strenuously denied through the pages of *Woman's Own* that his son, Andrew, had ever been a trouble, the lad's controversial affair with Koo Stark must have caused a few family problems at the time. And model Vicki Hodge's recollections of her and Andrew's nights of nude moonlit romps and love in the Carribean can't have gone down too well either. But the royal family have their own way of dealing with an embarrassing situation whether it be Princess Anne's speeding tickets or Andrew's affairs. Prince Philip may give the offender a dressing down, but after that, no one ever mentions it again.

There is no gossip, no chat, it is simply as if the incident has never occurred.

It is said that Philip's view regarding his sons has always been that they should sow their wild oats before they settle down, and that he has actively encouraged them to do just that.

But he does expect them to be discreet, as Charles always was, and he expects them to be discreet with the right kind of girl.

Koo, having appeared in a soft-porn movies without too many clothes on, was not exactly the right kind of girl. It was beside the point that she is, in fact, a rather charming and pleasant girl who was frequently unjustly treated by the Press (but then, who isn't!). She wasn't one of them and her background wouldn't do. The sad aspect of the affair was that the couple really did seem to care for each other. Andrew wanted to set up home with her and eventually marry her, which on the face of it, wasn't a very good idea.

Royal writer Andrew Morton says that Philip acted quickly when he realized the affair was getting serious. 'He summoned Andrew and told him he would like him to spend the weekend with him at Balmoral,' he says. 'As they walked through the Highland heather, Philip bluntly spelled out the facts of life to Andy. It was suggested that the couple should part for a while to see how strong their affection really was.'

Koo Stark went to Australia to think things over. Andrew was sent to the Caribbean with his ship, the HMS *Invincible*, and there he met the fun-loving, ex-nude model Vicki Hodge who helped a little to mend his broken heart.

Andrew Morton quotes a friend as saying: 'Quite simply, Andrew was nobbled by the system. Prince Philip won.'

As I said, he usually does.

A psychologist would no doubt explain that Philip acts the boss in the family because he has no authority elsewhere. It is because his role is unimportant in the outside world that he behaves like a heavy Victorian father. Children always have and always will rebel against a tough father, and all his sons have done just that.

And, of course, there aren't that many options open to his children other than the services. He once said that if his sons had not opted for the navy, then they would probably have been stuck with a church career.

Therefore the worst blow would have been when his youngest son, Edward, quit the Marines in January 1987 after only four months in the service. To quit is the worst crime in Philip's book, and for his son to fall out from the regiment for which the Duke is the Honorary Captain-General was hard to take. The disappointment in finding that his son did not have his father's 'undefeatable spirit' must have a severe blow to Philip's pride. It may not have occurred to him that to stand up to his father and quit could have required a lot more courage than sticking it out. And anyway, the lad didn't want join the Marines in the first place!

There was a furious family row, with Prince Philip telling his son to pull himself together and three hours of tears from Edward. It took the Queen to calm things down, arguing that what Edward needed was support from the family.

To make matters worse someone leaked a letter that Prince Philip had written to Commandant-General, Sir Michael Wilkins, head of the Marines. The letter expressed his regrets for what had happened, and it was handed to the *Sun* newspaper. To Philip's fury, the editor, Kelvin McKenzie, printed it. For once the Palace reacted and the *Sun*, having broken copyright, had to pay an undisclosed sum to a charity of Prince Philip's choosing.

But the four-million readers of the *Sun* had learned in the meantime that Philip had hoped to the bitter end that his son would change his mind. It was, he said, disappointing, but as usual, he managed to make the Press the scapegoat by remarking that the blaze of publicity had not helped.

And he was looking on the bright side when he said that at least Edward had had three years of the Marine training (including his time at University) which could only have done him good.

It didn't do the family relationship a great deal of good. At their shooting weekend when the news broke of Philip's letter, the Queen and the Duke had a furious public row at a pheasant shoot for local farmers.

The Queen was not in the best of moods with her husband, having been angry at the way he had handled the Edward crisis. She decided that he wasn't handling either the dogs or the arrangements for the shoot well, either, and accused him of bungling before storming off.

Edward has not yet redeemed himself in his father's eyes.

Philip was not exactly enchanted when Edward got himself involved in the farcical TV programme, 'It's a Knockout'. It might have all been for charity, but the fact that Edward coerced his brother, Andrew (plus Fergie) and his sister Anne into appearing on the programme and making fools of themselves did not help either. The programme was harmless enough, but lacking in dignity. Philip felt he could not stop Andrew's involvement if that's what he wanted to do, but he did not approve, and neither did the Queen. Prince Charles was appalled and Princess Margaret flatly refused to watch it.

So, like many a father in the land, Philip has had his disappointments with his sons. Perhaps because, like Charles, they decided that they, too, were not born to follow in their father's footsteps.

11

GOOD WORKS

No one could ever accuse the Duke of Edinburgh of not being a worker. He is always doing something; his excess of energy does not permit him to sit around doing nothing. But of all that he has done over the past forty years, the most worthwhile must surely be his work for the youth of Britain.

Over the years he has sponsored boys clubs, sailing clubs and raised cash to create playing fields. He has an instinctive sympathy for the young. He is genuinely interested in youth. And he has used his prodigious energy in raising enormous sums of money to make his far-seeing ideas work.

The best known of his projects is the Duke of Edinburgh's Award Scheme, the only one that bears his name.

When the Duke of Edinburgh's Award Scheme was proposed in 1954, critics said the concept was 'square'. Their opinion was that young people would never be interested in a scheme that encouraged leisure activities but with a view to developing a sense of service, fitness and purpose in their lives.

The critics were wrong. Today thousands and thousands of young people have joined the Award Scheme, either through their school, their employer or a youth organization. Over the years it has been an incredible success, and not just a middle-class one. Boys from borstals and detention centres have entered and found there was more in them than they knew. The scheme is classless, and for both boys and girls, aged from 14 up to 23.

This worthwhile concept has always been very expensive to run, and in its early days quickly ran into debt. In 1961 the scheme was £100,000 in the red; an enormous sum in those days. No bank would help and things looked black until the Duke himself came to the rescue. The tale of how he refunded his scheme tells more about the man than a recital of the endless good works he has been involved with over the past forty years. What he decided to do in order to get the awards back on the road was quite as startling and controversial as the younger members of his family's involvement with 'It's a Knockout'.

In 1961 James Carreras, now Sir James, was the first Briton to be president of Variety International. A marvellous genial man and a film maker of renown, he had come to know Philip vaguely in the late forties when Variety asked the Prince if he would attend a matinée in aid of the Great Ormond Street Hospital. Philip agreed and they saw each other occasionally over the next few years.

'Then I got this call asking if I could be at Buckingham Palace at six o'clock,' Sir James said. 'I walked in and there were three fellows in flying uniform. The Duke said to me: 'Do you think that if we went to America and did a tour we could raise some money for the Awards scheme?'

Sir James said he didn't know but he would find out from the Variety organization in the States, and then asked what sort of back-up the Prince could give him.

He said: 'I'll fly myself and I could probably spare about fourteen days.' He and his RAF friends were willing to go to Miami, Houston, Los Angeles, Chicago, New York and Toronto. And two years later they did just that.

'I rang up the chief barkers in the States who agreed it would be wonderful,' says Sir James. 'They reckoned they could put on a jolly good show and charge a lot of money, but they said not to forget they had their own charities to think about. The money would have to be split.

'We planned it, and came away most encouraged. They were going to charge about £100 a seat. We'd get about £100,000 and that would put the awards scheme right.

'It was a bit scary, the thought of spending fourteen days with Prince Philip. I've always been a little bit scared of him. There's a certain something that makes you hold back. We were only going to have him nights, during the day he was to attend meetings of the British Council and we'd pick him up about six o'clock at night. Each of the five centres were planning something top class. It wasn't going to be crappy. It was looking good.

'So then we had the good idea of all the hosts from the five centres coming over with their wives to meet the Duke of Edinburgh. They couldn't get on the plane fast enough. That meant he knew them all before he went there. And in 1963 the trip started and I must say it was a sensational success. I don't think the States had seen Prince Philip before, and I don't think he had seen such weird people in all his life. It was quite remarkable. He was wonderful. So nice, except on certain occasions . . .'

The Prince piloted himself, and Sir James was at each centre five hours before him, making sure everything was ready. It wasn't all plain sailing. Variety Club were given a list of instructions from the Palace as to what must NOT happen. He was not to be introduced to girls with hour-glass contours; they went so far as to get the bra-size of every girl he was to meet! Top-line entertainers, including Frank Sinatra, gave their services free but there were some nasty moments when strangers ran up and seized him by the hand and others shouted 'Hallo, Phil,' which didn't go down a treat.

'There were some bumpy moments,' said Sir James. 'He was always in a filthy temper at breakfast time, and in Los Angeles there was a special cocktail party for about forty or fifty people who had all paid $1,000 each. The director of Variety came up to me and said: 'There are thirty ladies who will each donate another $1,000 each if the Duke will shake hands with them.' When I told him, he gave me a filthy look and said: 'Oh, all right.' He opened the door and you wouldn't believe it. They were all dressed in white and they were all wearing Prince of Wales feathers—all thirty of them. He went round the lot and thirty seconds later he was out!

'When we arrived in Miami it was very hot and he said he wanted a swim. Well, we couldn't put him in the hotel pool with five hundred other people there. But there was a woman who lived opposite who said if he'd swim in her pool she'd give $10,000 to the charity. He went across, swam in her pool and spent a very nice afternoon. But she never paid up. We couldn't pressurise her.

143

'It was a unique trip. The Los Angeles banquet and show was out of this world. The only thing we had to do was sit him next to stars . . . the top elegant ones. No birds. If we'd done that we'd have been dead, executed.

'The most embarrassing of all was the day we were going to 20th Century Fox. I saw young Daryl Zanuck and asked what he was going to do. They planned to give a really wonderful lunch on one of the big sound stages and bring all the big stars and make a couple of speeches. I thought it was going to be fine.

'As we approached the studio, I thought: "Jesus!" There were about forty-eight cowboys on horses, and they all surrounded the car firing revolvers.

'I thought you said we were going to have lunch?' said the Duke, and all of a sudden there was a great shout and one of those bloody great stage-coaches arrives. A bird with big tits gets out and says: "Come in, Sir." "Not bloody likely!" he said.

'We moved two beauties who weren't actresses who were supposed to be sitting next to him, and then in the middle of lunch these fellows were firing revolvers as a sort of cabaret. He hated it, and he hated me, I tell you, so we left before we were due to go.

'When we got to the car he saw an enormous sound stage where Dean Martin and Jerry Lewis were working. "Are they filming in there?" he asked. We went in and he had the most hilarious afternoon, impromptu, and it saved the day.'

It was, says Sir James, a rough tour. Philip had no time to himself.

'It was a unique episode for him. He had been everywhere but he had never been alone like this, surrounded by strangers. Normally the Queen is with him, and if he's alone it's all embassies and ambassadors. But this was idiots like me.

But he never said much. Afterwards, when we presented him with the cheque for £100,000, the Queen was charming. I was a little nervous about that because I thought she might say there was something we shouldn't have done. Apparently we did it all right, but God, we didn't half work at it for three years!

'I never had a letter from him at all. Nothing until the dinner when the cheque was presented. At the dinner he had no idea how much we had raised. There was a two month gap between our return and the dinner and I'd heard nothing. But when I handed over the cheque he gave me a pair of cuff-links with his crest on.

'But he's not one for giving you a great deal of encouragement. He doesn't give pats on the back.

'But it was worth it for the scheme. It's a bloody good thing, I tell you. To see the gold awards presented makes you very proud. And everyone who receives one is a better citizen. It's grown so big now that he couldn't possible present all the medals himself.

'The awards scheme is very special to him. He can be almost inspirational, you know. There's something about him that makes you bloody well want to do it. Why did I want to go to American and kill myself with all that work? But there was something about him. I couldn't say no. And I've always been glad that I didn't.'

12

A FORTUNATE MAN

In a 1969 poll run by *The Daily Telegraph* to discover who the British thought would make the best dictator, Prince Philip won. Enoch Powell was a close second.

The result must have given him a few wistful moments of fantasizing about what he would do should he really be in charge. There are no prizes for surmising that the first casualties under his regime would be the Press.

Philip has never come to terms with the media, and since he is, to use his own vernacular, always so bloody rude to them, it gives them some pleasure to irritate him in return. It is true he gets treated with scant courtsey. The Queen Mother, who could give him a lesson or two, winds the Press around her little finger. Prince Philip makes them as bolshie and bloody-minded as he is himself.

At a glittering reception in Trinidad he turned on reporters and to their astonishment snarled: 'You have ruined my life.'

Ruined his life? Oh, come on! With £209,300 from the civil list in 1987, with all those homes and all those holidays—six weeks in Sandringham in the winter, ten weeks in Balmoral in the summer, every weekend off at Windsor, and plenty of time for practising carriage-driving midweek? It would take some ruining!

He has nothing as sordid as money problems. The Prince has cars, planes, helicopters and boats that he can whistle up whenever he wants them. Once, when he wanted to get from Holy Island for a polo game in Windsor, he whistled up a naval launch, a destroyer, a car, a Heron of the Queen's flight and another car at the other end. He arrived on time, and the taxpayer footed the travel bill. He was outraged when the Press said this was all a bit much for a game of polo.

He doesn't have too many overheads yet he complains a lot about money. Presumably what is the Queen's is his. Certainly it will one day be their children's. The Queen is probably the richest woman in the world and she pays no tax. Imagine the roll-on effect of all that money, wisely invested and no tax on the interest.

Then there are the little perks. Every time Philip goes on an overseas tour, we, the taxpayer, buy him a new wardrobe. It's unlikely he's ever paid for a suit in his life out of his own money. His orderlies are both from the army, so the main part of their salary is paid by the Ministry of Defence. Around seventy-five per cent of the expenses incurred in running the monarchy are paid by the Departmental Appropriations—and that means the British tax-payer. And those appropriations do not include the civil list.

Not a bad old life, one might say.

Britain likes its monarchy and few begrudge him. But Prince Philip's problem is that he is not only paranoid about the Press (who admittedly can be quite as nasty as he can be) but that his arrogance has never let him come to terms with a simple truth—that there is a price to pay for everything in life. And the price in Philip's case for the luxurious existence he enjoys is that if he takes his taxfree £209,300 from the taxpayer, the latter has some right to know what he is up to. He and his family are of enormous interest to a public hungry for every detail of their lives. There-fore, he and his family are of enormous interest to the Press — because they sell newspapers. If Britain wasn't monarchy-minded, he would get all the solitude he craves. But Heaven help him if that interest goes. He might not get his £209,300 any more. He did once say they'd go quietly if that was what the public wanted. Unthinkable, but should it happen, with their own private money and possessions they'd be about a million miles and a few million pounds from the breadline.

But if there's one thing that monarchy can't abide, it's people making money out of them. It's true to say that they do make profits for the media. In Philip's perfect world he would have all of the privileges with none of the publicity.

The war with Fleet Street began on his honeymoon. Pestered by both public and press, he drove out of Broadlands, the honeymoon home, dangerously fast, scattering the pressmen who were waiting outside. He once went so far as to pepper a reporter's car with shotgun pellets at Sandringham. Less dangerous but no more endearing were comments like: 'Which are the apes and which are the reporters?' when he was feeding the Barbary apes at Gibraltar. He once saw a Pakistani photographer fall out of a tree and remarked: 'I hope to God he breaks his bloody neck!' In South American he said: 'You have mosquitoes, I have the Press.'

One could fill several pages of this book with Philip's quips of this nature. Or indeed a whole chapter if one repeated his doubtful wit and wisdom delivered to local and foreign dignitaries, sometimes indeed to whole countries. Remember how he upset the Chinese with his cracks about slitty eyes? And not for the first time. The only other time he went that far east he had a go at them for grinding up the horns of the rhinoceros as an aphrodisiac. The Chinese denied it.

Sometimes the biter gets bitten. When he cracked at a be-medalled South American general that he hadn't realized Brazil had been in the war that long, the general had the last word.

'At least I didn't get them for marrying my wife,' he said coldly.

The Mayor of Calgary was another who was not going to be put down. When he presented Philip with a stetson hat, the Duke pulled a face and groaned. 'Not another one!' he said. 'Oh well, I suppose I can use it for a pot.'

Later the Mayor presented his royal guest with a spread of antlers.

'Don't ask me what to do with them, and I won't tell you where to stick them,' he said.

Prince Philip believes in calling a spade a spade (and he probably would, too, if he felt like it). He is all too often a most undiplomatic consort. But one must not forget the thousands and thousands of appearances he has made where he has never put a foot wrong. This is the routine boring stuff of royalty that never gets reported.

'He does not suffer fools gladly, and is impatient with what he considers stupidity,' said a man who has frequently felt the rough side of his tongue. 'When he encounters either, he is rude. Sometimes abusive. Often he is just rude anyway. The pity is that a man of his wit and intelligence should find it necessary to put people down so brutally. It would show more style if he picked on targets of his own weight or at least ones who could answer back.'

Before Michael Parker left his employment in 1957, Parker told his dear 'Pippo' that he would really have to come to terms with the Press and improve the relationship between himself and Fleet Street. Philip has never achieved this, and now probably never will.

But he has achieved a great deal more. Like the man or loathe him, he has tried to earn his corn over the past forty years. And in spite of 'the bloody press', he is a fortunate man in that he has been able to enjoy himself while doing so.

The most painful sacrifice he had to make for his chosen life was to deny his family. His sisters and their families were banned from the wedding. It was many years before the Queen quietly met them on their home ground. Over the years Prince Philip has regularly slipped out of Britain to stay with them. When he was younger, he went for the wild-boar hunting on their huge estates. Even all these years after the war, their visits to Britain are always private; never publicized. The Queen Mother does not care for what she calls 'the German relations'. And his German background has always been played down. It's curious to think that Princes Charles has fourteen German first cousins who are unknown, and never mentioned in Britain.

Prince Philip's mother did spend the last few years of her life quietly at Buckingham Palace. She wore a nun's habit, ate mostly grapes and not a lot else, and chain-smoked. Palace servants always knew when she was about by the cough! She was wheeled about in Queen Mary's old wheelchair by the Duke's pages. A true eccentric, when she died in December 1969, she was 84, and buried at Windsor where she had been born.

In his lifetime Prince Philip has travelled an extraordinary number of miles, delivered uncounted speeches—though his computerized filing system could probably tell us how many—and involved himself in many good works, mostly fund-raising for various charities near to his heart. He has modernized the monarchy so that it is now more popular than it has ever been. (Making, one might say, a rod for his own back.) He has made some brilliant, pertinent speeches that reveal a deeply thoughful man whose heart and values appear to be in the right place. Other speeches, when he felt qualified to tell us all what to do—and when does he not feel qualified to tell us what to do?—gave the impression that he had the whole nation lined up on the quarter deck for inspection. However, he is not an 'insensitive clod' as some describe him, nor is he an 'ignorant bum' as he once described himself. His whole life has been dedicated to the pursuit of knowledge.

He is an organizer, an inventor, an artist of some skill, and a thinker. He is the 20th-century man who can sail a yacht, command a ship, fly a jet, ride a horse, shoot a stag. There's not a lot he can't do. He has interested himself in science, management, conservation, space and the future and knows enough about them all to ask the right questions. He asks a lot of questions. He also has an annoying habit of telling experts a way to do it better.

But somewhere in amongst that collection of admirable qualities there is also an angry, impatient man who isn't always under control. A man who is obsessed with being top dog. He releases his anger on the unwary and the stupid just as he used to release it on his polo ponies, riding them to the point of cruelty in his determination to win. Today he is equally tough on his carriage horses. The pity is that for a time the outlet for this ever-present anger was his eldest son.

It poses the question: Can this be a happy man?

When he first married the Queen he tried to be the breadwinner and quickly found it impossible. Perhaps he resents taking his £209,300 a year from us. Perhaps he wishes he would earn it for himself. It must be hard for the superior man who also has an unfortunate—and unnecessary—superiority complex to accept that all he has comes second hand.

It also poses the question of where he would be today if he had not married the Queen? Had his father's family won the battle for control of him when he was a child he would have been brought up in Nazi Germany, and a marriage to the Princess Elizabeth would have been unthinkable. In the tradition of his father's family he would probably have married a wealthy woman, a German princess maybe, and be enjoying shooting wild boar (one of his favourite pastimes) on a German estate without the attentions of the Press to remind him of the paradox of the conservationist who kills. Or he could have just remained another piece of European royal flotsam doggedly calling himself Prince and clinging to past glories.

Unlikely, this, with his God-given energy.

As it is, Prince Philip has fathered the future king of England and begun his own dynastic line. His place in history is secure.

He is a fortunate man.

BIBLIOGRAPHY

Alexandra, Queen. *Prince Philip: A Family Portrait* Hodder & Stoughton, 1959

Baillie-Grohman, Vice-Admiral Harold Tom. *Naval Anthology*, Vol. II. Unpublished

Boothroyd, J.B. *Philip: An Informal Biography* Longman, 1971

Channon, Sir Henry ('Chips'). *The Diaries of Sir Henry Channon MP* (ed. R.R.James) Weidenfeld & Nicolson, 1967

Clark, Brigadier Stanley. *Palace Diary* Harrap, 1958

Cordet, Helene. *Born Bewildered*. Peter Davies, 1961

Crawford, M. *The Little Princess* Cassell, 1950

Dean, J. *HRH Prince Philip: A Portrait by his Valet* Robert Hale,

Fisher, Graham and Heather. *Consort, the Life and Times of Prince Philip* W.H. Allen, 1980

Frischauer, Willi. *Margaret, Princess without a Cause* Michael Joseph, 1977

Hollis, Sir Leslie. *The Captain General* Herbert Jenkins, 1961

Judd, Dennis, *Prince Philip: A Biography* Michael Joseph, 1980

Lacey, R. *Majesty* Hutchinson, 1977

Lane, Peter. *Prince Philip* Robert Hale, 1980

Liversidge, D. *Prince Philip* Andrew Barker, 1976

Parker, Eileen. *Step Aside for Royalty* Bachman & Turner, 1982

Purcell, William. *Fisher of Lambeth, a Portrait from Life* Hodder & Stoughton, 1969

Summers, Anthony, and Stephen Dorril. *Honeytrap: The Secret Worlds of Stephen Ward* Weidenfeld & Nicolson, 1987

Townsend, P. *Time and Chance* Collins, 1978

Wheeler-Bennett, Sir John. *King George VI* Macmillan, 1958

INDEX